XAVIER BEKAERT | GILLIS JONK
JAN RAES | PHEBO WIBBENS

# ICONIC

HOW TO CREATE A VIRTUOUS
CIRCLE OF SUCCESS

Published by
**LID Publishing Limited**
One Adam Street, London WC2N 6LE

31 West 34th Street, 8th Floor, Suite 8004,
New York, NY 10001, U.S.

info@lidpublishing.com
www.lidpublishing.com

A member of:

**BPR**
Business Publishers Roundtable
**www.businesspublishersroundtable.com**

© Xavier Bekaert, Gillis Jonk, Jan Raes and Phebo Wibbens, 2016
© LID Publishing Limited, 2016

Printed in Great Britain by TJ International
ISBN: 978-1-910649-76-3

Cover and page design: Caroline Li

XAVIER BEKAERT | GILLIS JONK
JAN RAES | PHEBO WIBBENS

# ICONIC

## HOW TO CREATE A VIRTUOUS CIRCLE OF SUCCESS

LID

LONDON       MONTERREY
MADRID       SHANGHAI
MEXICO CITY  BOGOTA
NEW YORK     BUENOS AIRES
BARCELONA    SAN FRANCISCO

# CONTENTS

# INTRODUCTION

It takes only two things to become an icon:

A.  Be the admired leader in your field
B.  Do so longer than deemed possible

Yet the vast majority of organizations never get there. A select few however do, and when they do, they often manage to do so for half a century, a century or more. This begs the question why, and how do they pull this off?

This book is about icons. Not the works of art commonly found in Eastern Orthodox churches, but exceptional organizations: leading orchestras, Michelin-starred restaurants, teams of world-renowned surgeons, invincible sports teams or stellar companies. All of them have an aspiration to make or do something special, and to go on doing so, year in, year out for decades. This is what gives these organizations their undeniable iconic status.

The one that grabbed our attention, and that set the writing of this book in motion, was Amsterdam's Royal Concertgebouw Orchestra (RCO). In 2013, the RCO celebrated its 125th anniversary. It rose to prominence only a few years after its founding, and has maintained a leadership position ever since. Such an astonishing feat deserves explanation, and that's why we decided to find out how the Concertgebouw Orchestra and other iconic organizations like it manage to stay at the top of their field for so long.

The Concertgebouw Orchestra shared our enthusiasm for this question, and invited us to research it in detail. In fact, managing director of the Royal Concertgebouw Orchestra **Jan Raes** joined the research efforts and author team. Raes had at that time already been managing director of the RCO for a number of years and had led various cultural institutions in the Netherlands and Belgium, and felt privileged now to be part of this orchestra. He was curious to understand what made the Concertgebouw Orchestra so special.

We quickly found out that the RCO is driven by a virtuous circle of competence which enables it to sustain its growth and continue to produce amazing results. Further research into other leading orchestras and iconic organizations revealed that they are all driven by a similar circle of competence.

This circle is stunning in its simplicity and in what it tells us about how organizations like this remain icons: their outstanding performance attracts the best *talent*, and with these people, they are able to form high-performing *teams* that are driven by absolute aspiration and can go on to achieve unparalleled results over *time*. In this way, the circle becomes self-sustaining. If it can be maintained by creating the right conditions, the organization can, in the fullness of time, become iconic. And as it turns out, such a circle of iconic competence can be incredibly robust. Although each organization interprets the elements of the circle of competency in its own way, the elements remain the same. As if to prove this point, one of our interviewees at the Berlin Philharmonic actually thought that we had based the circle of competence on his own orchestra.

This book has not been written in the form of a scientific report. Instead, and in order to do justice to the iconic organizations we have studied, we have tried to transmit the almost tangible sense of inspiration that we felt during our research and in the conversations we had with the members of those organizations. We hope to lead you on an insightful journey through iconic organizations, revealing the circle of iconic competence, and showing you how it applies in practice.

We wrote this book first and foremost for executives and managers with a leadership responsibility, to give them a sense of inspiration which they can pass on to their organizations. But this book will also be of interest for anyone who wants to take a look behind the scenes of some of the world's best-performing orchestras, restaurants, sports teams and companies.

There is arguably no particularly suitable timing for writing a book about iconic organizations that are around for decades or even more than a century. And indeed, the ideas and concepts for this book have been in the back of our minds and the subject of our intermittent research efforts for many years.

Jan and **Xavier Bekaert** met by chance after a concert in the Concertgebouw, and decided to continue their conversation. They quickly realised that there were many more similarities than they had first thought between orchestras and, for example, the management consulting firms that Xavier had first hand experience with. Strict selection of people, pure meritocracy, distributed leadership, an aspiration to constantly exceed expectations; all these things resulted in a positive feedback loop of success, and one which seemed surprisingly similar in all the iconic organizations they were familiar with. And so the idea for a book about iconic organizations was born.

A shared passion for deeply understanding organizations brought the entire author team together. Between us we have many years of strategy consulting experience at A.T. Kearney, Bain & Company, and Benthurst & Co which has given us the privilege of working closely with a large variety of organizations. It also fueled our natural desire to truly understand a given situation and distill the most pertinent learnings for broader application. Both **Gillis Jonk** and **Phebo Wibbens** have for example prior experience in developing and writing about strategic concepts at A.T. Kearney and Bain & Company respectively.

The ideas in this book came about during interviews with leaders and in lengthy discussions within its team of authors. They form the synthesis of our research into the 14 iconic organizations discussed in this book.

Dealing with members of iconic organizations and exchanging ideas with them has been a source of great personal inspiration for us, and has generated many new insights. We hope to share them with you.

**Xavier Bekaert**, **Gillis Jonk**,
**Jan Raes** and **Phebo Wibbens**

# FOREWORD

My first encounter with the Royal Concertgebouw Orchestra (RCO) dates back more then 60 years, to when I first joined my parents at the Concertgebouw for the famous "Beethoven Cycle". From 1922 to 1957, the RCO performed Beethoven symphonies at the end of the regular season. Although my memories of these concerts are mixed (as an eight-year-old I thought them to be very long), I had the extreme fortune to hear Beethoven's masterpieces performed under legendary conductors like Otto Klemperer, Pierre Monteux, Bruno Walter, Eugen Jochum, and, of course, the chief conductor at the time, Eduard van Beinum. This experience has laid the foundations of my profound love for music and for the RCO, which culminated in the honour of my becoming a member of its board nearly 50 years later, and subsequently in the privilege of being one of its ambassadors.

The orchestra is a fantastic example of the importance of excellence, which is the subject of this book. The RCO has reached such prominence because it has always pursued a number of basic principles that can easily be translated into the corporate world: teamwork, high standards, strong leadership, meritocracy and rigorous talent development are some of the characteristics that made the RCO what it is today.

The orchestra is a group of more than 120 members, and each one of them is the best in their profession. To make a well-oiled organization from these highly talented individuals is a remarkable accomplishment of the management and the chief conductor. Their dedication and the superb quality of the members create a true team that strives for excellence and an environment where individual performance is an integral part of the success of the group.

This book analyses this remarkable accomplishment and compares it with those of other iconic institutions, such as El Bulli and the All Blacks, to name but two examples . The authors also develop a model that comprises a number of features common to the organizations discussed in the book. It is a useful read for anyone who would like to apply the tools that lead to iconic success in their own business environment.

Amsterdam, October 2015

**Tom de Swaan**
Chairman Zurich Insurance Group

CHAPTER 1
# MAGIC ON DEMAND

Led by Jean-Louis Neichel (right) elBulli got his first Michelin star in 1976

This chapter introduces the most important topics and examples that will be discussed in the book. We will demonstrate the magic that the output of iconic organizations can invoke, and present the virtuous circle of competence that icons manage to sustain over the course of several decades or even a century. The chapter is concluded with a brief overview of the book's structure and a list of the organizations studied.

# The Magic of a Concert

On 17 February 2010, the Royal Concertgebouw Orchestra (RCO) performed Gustav Mahler's Third Symphony at New York's Carnegie Hall. The composer wrote this symphony "as a glorification of existence", wrote *The New York Times*.[1] "A performance led with the passion, energy and sense of mystical otherworldliness the score demands will inevitably push the musicians to their limits." A true test, therefore, of the orchestra's mettle.

Earlier that day, first violinist Christian van Eggelen had attended a reception held in a private room by board members of a sponsor who would be present at the concert that evening.[2] Van Eggelen said a few words about the coming performance, and asked if anyone had ever heard a Mahler symphony before. Only one of those present raised his hand – most had had little experience of classical music. Van Eggelen began to worry if this really was the most suitable concert for this kind of audience to listen to: over an hour and a half of heavy, classical music, with no interval.

That evening, chief conductor Mariss Jansons took to the podium to loud applause and, in the silence that followed, Van Eggelen felt the tensions rise. Seconds seemed like minutes. Then the eight French horns began to play as one; out of nothing, the sound was pure and even. And Van Eggelen knew that this was going to be another magical evening, an evening when everything would be just right. By the time the sound of the horns died away at the end of the opening theme, the enchantment was complete. Mahler requires the French horn players to play *pianissimo*, then *morendo*: as softly as they possibly can, and then more softly still, the sound literally 'dying away'. Playing this softly demands a great deal of courage from a French horn player. Even the slightlest hesitation in their lips can cause the instrument to shift to another note. But that did not happen on an evening as magical as this. The horns died away to the edge of audibility.

---

[1] Allan Kozinn (2010). 'A Dutch Orchestra Plumbing the Depths'. *New York Times*, 18 February.

[2] Anecdote told by Christian van Eggelen in interview with Phebo Wibbens, Amsterdam, 24 October 2012.

Nobody knew why, but everybody agreed: this was a special evening. The musicians felt on top of the world and played to the best of their ability. Adrenaline coursed through Van Eggelen's veins. *This* was why he played for the Concertgebouw Orchestra, and it was an addictive feeling. The audience, too, clearly seemed to feel the magic. Not even a cough or a sniffle. Then the final note sounded to thunderous applause. People had tears in their eyes. Once the concert was over, Van Eggelen went to the sponsor's reception, where he was greeted by a very different scene to the one he had left that afternoon: gone were the tight-lipped executives; in their place a joyous and adoring crowd. Now, at last, they understood why people listen to classical music.

"Mr. Jansons's Mahler made the Sibelius and Rachmaninoff works on the Tuesday program seem like curtain raisers," wrote *The New York Times*, "although on their own those performances had considerable strengths."

# Iconic Organizations

Why is it that one concert is magical, while another is just very good? This is *not* a question we will attempt to answer in this book, for its explanation lies hidden in the intangible mystery of the creative process. What we will do instead is show how an organization can create a set of conditions that, in combination, can work magic time after time, and in doing so, can make it into an icon.

The Royal Concertgebouw Orchestra, which celebrated its 125th birthday in 2013, is just such an icon. Along with the Philharmonic Orchestras of Berlin and Vienna, it is generally considered to be among the world's top three, and in 2008 was awarded the title of "the world's greatest orchestra" by the *Gramophone* music magazine (see *Figure 1-1*).

1. Royal Concertgebouw Orchestra (Amsterdam)
2. Berlin Philharmonic
3. Vienna Philharmonic
4. London Symphony Orchestra
5. Chicago Symphony Orchestra
6. Bavarian Radio Symphony Orchestra (Munich)
7. Cleveland Orchestra
8. Los Angeles Philharmonic
9. Budapest Festival Orchestra
10. Staatskapelle Dresden
11. Boston Symphony Orchestra
12. New York Philharmonic
13. San Francisco Symphony Orchestra
14. Mariinsky Theatre Orchestra
15. Russian National Orchestra
16. Saint Petersburg Philharmonia
17. The Gewandhaus Orchestra Leipzig
18. Metropolitan Opera Orchestra
19. Saito Kinen Orchestra
20. Czech Philharmonic Orchestra

**Figure 1-1**   Top 20 orchestras according to the Gramophone magazine, based on a survey of 12 editors worldwide.

Its iconic status dates back to the time of Willem Mengelberg, who was chief conductor[3] from 1895 to 1945. Famous composers including Edvard Grieg, Gustav Mahler, Claude Debussy, Richard Strauss, Arnold Schönberg and Igor Stravinsky chose the RCO to premier their latest compositions. Some of these great composers even conducted their works in person[4].

What is so special about the Royal Concertgebouw Orchestra? Herman Rieken, percussionist with the RCO, puts it like this: "In every concert, we seek to push ourselves to the limits of our ability. We always try to play the best we can and often something magical happens." Lead bassist Dominic Seldis agrees: "I've played in a number of different orchestras, and there will usually be two or three times a year when you hit the sweet spot, when you play a concert when everything goes just right. In the RCO, we try to hit the sweet spot every single night. Everybody gets completely intoxicated when we do, and disappointed if we don't. That's the difference."

A passion for perfection is someting we see time and time again in organizations that have achieved iconic status in their field. Take the restaurant elBulli as an example:[5] "Going to eat in an avant-garde restaurant, gives you something like a creative emotion. It's not just about 'Mmm, tastes good.' You feel something. You think, 'Killer!'. For us, the emotional element has always been more important."

That magic can only be achieved with a single-minded focus on quality. "It's not as if you wake up one morning with a good idea, and then you're done," says elBulli's chef Ferran Adrià. "You find out how hard it is to be creative day in, day out." Until its temporary closure in 2011[6], elBulli was only open for six months a year. The other six months were spent focusing completely on developing and perfecting new dishes. The restaurant served a different menu of 35 dishes each week for about 50 guests every evening and employed 60 service staff, including 40 chefs.[7]

Former chief conductor of the RCO Mariss Jansons says: "If you want to go up into space, you need a three-stage rocket. The first two stages take up by far the most energy. Then all you need at the third stage is one last spurt to escape gravity. Music is no different: you have to work really hard to achieve technical perfection of the highest quality, and then you need something extra to create the magic."

---

[3]  Mengelberg's offical title at the time of his appointment was 'Musical Director'.

[4]  L. Samama (1989). 'De woelige jaren (1895-1920)' (p. 102). In H.J. van Royen et al. (ed.). *Historie en kroniek van het Concertgebouw en het Concertgebouworkest*, Deel 1. Zutphen: De Walburg Pers.

[5]  Gereon Wetzel (2012). 'elBulli: Cooking in Progress'. *Alive Mind* [dvd].

[6]  elBulli voluntarily closed its restaurant and is transforming itself into a culinary thinktank.

[7]  Michael Norton, Julian Villanueva & Luc Wathieu (2009). *elBulli: The Taste of Innovation*. Harvard Business School case study.

This striving for the extraordinary may not seem directly applicable in a business setting. And yet in iconic organizations, we do see a striving for perfect quality and then a bit more on top: nobody who has held an iPad for the first time would claim it's just another piece of consumer electronics. Or take Lego, which over the course of 60 years has grown into an icon in children's toys. *"Det bedste er ikke for godt"* - "Even the best is not good enough" was the motto of Lego's founder Ole Kirk Christiansen.

Even a company like IKEA has a knack for seeking to surpass perfection, even though this may not be in simple terms of product quality. IKEA's vision is "to make better everyday lives for the masses by offering a wide range of well-designed, functional home furnishing products at prices so low that as many people as possible will be able to afford them".[8] IKEA lives up to its motto. The company has sold over 50 million units of its most iconic product, the Billy bookcase. Perhaps even more remarkable is that the Billy, after correction for inflation, is now 76% cheaper than it was when it was introduced 30 years ago.[9] It is the culmination of 30 years of striving for perfection: every screw is in just the right place, every part has been developed so that it fits into the smallest possible packaging, and the thickness of each shelf strikes just the right balance between strength and weight. The Billy has thus achieved a certain level of beauty.

Sport, too, bears witness to the enormous drive of iconic teams. "For us, losing a game hurts just as much as losing a family member," says a former captain of New Zealand's national rugby team the All Blacks, a team that is feared as much as it is revered. This team is iconic in all it does. Each game begins with a *haka*, or traditional Maori war dance. The enormous ambition that is invested in this dance is not without consequence: over the 111 years of the team's existence, the All Blacks have won twice as many points as their opponents, and won 75% of their matches. In recent years, this figure has increased to 87%. Compare this with a mere 63% of matches won by the Brazilian national football team, praised by so many. With fewer than 4.5 million inhabitants, New Zealand has held the number-one spot in world rugby for longer than all other countries combined, including much larger nations such as South Africa, Australia and England.

The Royal Concertgebouw Orchestra, elBulli, the All Blacks; they are all teams that are determined to leave an extraodinary and lasting legacy. Emeritus Professor of Sociology Anton Zijderveld wrote of the team spirit that can be generated in this way: "It's a feeling of complete identification, of radical unity, of exaltation, even – a true mystical union. We see this in religious communities, in patriotic and nationalistic demonstrations and, less emotionally, much more soberly, in all forms of teamwork. The aesthetic experience, such as making music together, could also be added to this list: if they respond to each other well, the members of a jazz combo or a string quartet can sense exactly what the others want and what they will do next. It's as if a single individual is making the music."[10]

Here is what we want to understand: how does an iconic organization get its individual team members to play together in a way that produces such outstanding results? The question is the same regardless of whether we are talking about music, sport, consumer electronics, strategic consulting, or any other discipline.

# The Circle of Iconic Competence

*Good is the enemy of great*, wrote the management guru Jim Collins.[11] Most organizations already count themselves lucky if they manage to deliver products or services that are "good enough". But many do not succeed even in doing that. We find design hotels with fabulous rooms but unhelpful receptionists; TVs with amazing screen resolution but an impenetrable menu structure; extremely economical cars with satellite navigation systems that take us on circuitous routes … there are few organizations that pursue and achieve really exemplary quality.

8   Ingvar Kamprad. *The Testament of a Furniture Dealer*. Inter IKEA Systems B.V., 2007.
9   Chris Zook & James Allen (2012). *Repeatability: Build Enduring Businesses for a World of Constant Change*. Boston: Harvard Business Review Press.
10  Anton C. Zijderveld (1998). De samenleving als schouwspel. Boom. Bert Koopman, journalist with *Het Financieele Dagblad*, pointed us to this quote.
11  Jim Collins (2001). *Good to Great*. HarperCollins.

There are even fewer organizations that manage to sustain their exemplary quality over a number of leadership generations. A look back at the study *In Search of Excellence* clearly shows how hard it is to hold on to success.[12] This headline-grabbing book from the early 1980s shared "lessons learned from America's best-run companies", based on 62 companies which met a number of criteria for "long-term" excellence. Some of the companies studied are still big names (IBM, Intel, McDonalds, Procter & Gamble), but others have lost their former iconic status (Eastman Kodak, Xerox). Still others have been taken over (Digital Equipment, Wang Labs, K-Mart) or have gone bust (Polaroid, General Motors). This has nothing to do with the quality of the book's research, but with the fact that success, for most organizations, is a very fleeting experience.

Even the leading companies founded by Steve Jobs, Apple and Pixar, are experiencing (temporary) difficulties, now that their visionary leader is no more.[13] After the Apple Maps debacle, Apple lost some customer trust. Since then, the company has not introduced any new innovations to equal the iPod, iTunes, the iMac, the iPhone or the iPad – although it may still yet do so.[14] Pixar, too, appears to be having difficulty in maintaining its lead. Between 1995 and 2010, films produced by the studio were without exception met with universal acclaim. Six of the ten Oscars for best animation film between 2001 and 2010 went to Pixar, and ten of the eleven films produced by the studio score higher than 80% on the *Rotten Tomatoes* web site, which records the percentage of a movie's reviews that are positive. However, after 2010 less than half the films that Pixar has produced have achieved this score (see *Figure. 1-2*).

---

[12]  T. Peters & R.H. Waterman Jr. (1982). *In Search of Excellence: Lessons from America's Best-Run Companies*. Harper & Row.

[13]  It is too early to make final judgement on Apple and Pixar. As we shall see in Chapter 6, it is not unusual for an organization to experience a crisis when its visonary, founding father or group of leaders disappears. Many organizations never recover. Some do, and in time they can become iconic.

[14]  Despite accounting for well over half of the fast growing smart watch sales, at the moment Apple's iWatch doesn't seem to elicit the same breakthrough emotions as the products launched under Steve Jobs.

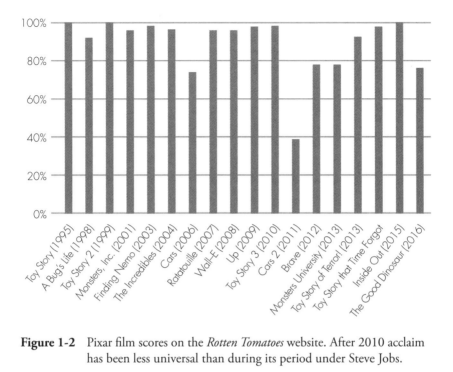

**Figure 1-2**  Pixar film scores on the *Rotten Tomatoes* website. After 2010 acclaim has been less universal than during its period under Steve Jobs.

The same applies to orchestras. Most orchestras that make it to the top do so under the leadership of a single conductor; once he leaves, they sink back into mediocrity. The RCO is a notable exception; under the leadership of five successive chief conductors since Mengelberg, it has always managed to reaffirm its status as a top international orchestra.

How has the Concertgebouw Orchestra succeeded in maintaining its success for so long, when most other organizations have seen their glory come and go? One obvious explanation is that organizations that are successful in the long term – whether by luck or design – simply face fewer problems along the way. But that is not true of the RCO. Anyone who opens the history books will see that crises arose in almost every decade of its existence. In 1904, for instance, barely 16 years after its founding, a conflict arose that would go down in the history books as "the Concertgebouw conflict", spanning the various relationships between the concert hall, the director, and his musicians. The orchestra's business manager, Willem Hutschenruyter, became involved in a heated difference of opinions with its music director, Mengelberg, and was eventually forced to leave. With him left a number of prominent members of the orchestra, including the first concertmaster, first cellist, solo flutist and solo trumpet player.[15] In one way or another, similar conflicts would recur at regular intervals throughout the century that followed.

Furthermore, the transitions to new chief conductors were, more often than not, difficult periods. Some of them were even dramatic; Mengelberg's forced departure after the war due to his Nazi sympathies, the sudden death of Van Beinum, who died of a cardiac arrest during an orchestral rehearsal. Nonetheless, the quality of music was sustained throughout each crisis. Apparently, there was "something" that gave the RCO as an organization the resilience to recover time and again.

To find out what that special something is, we spoke to more than 20 people involved in the RCO, including musicians, conductors, managers, support staff and journalists. We also looked at two other orchestras that, for more than a century, have also stayed at the top: the Berlin and the Vienna Philharmonic. All the three orchestras are clearly and recognisably different in terms of their unique sound and playing culture. And yet we found striking similarities in the resilience of their organizations when we studied how they were able to maintain their edge. We were even more surprised to learn that the forces that allow these orchestras to maintain their iconic status were similar to those found in, for example, the top restaurant elBulli, or in other, more prosaic examples we will encounter in business, such as Shell, Danaher and McKinsey.

We measured the iconic status of the organizations we studied based on their long-term results: icons are organizations that are admired leaders in their fields and that continue to be so for longer than is generally believed possible. In other words, conspicuously long periods of admiration make organizations iconic. We have deliberately chosen not to define iconic status in terms of financial or other directly measurable results, because iconicity is almost always a subjective concept, just like there is no clear way of measuring how good a concert is. Nevertheless, our definition can be applied objectively. Virtually every lover of classical music will rank the RCO, along with the Vienna and Berlin Philharmonics, among the most

---

[15]  Samama (1989).

iconic orchestras of the past hundred years. In the same way, almost every rugby enthusiast will view the All Blacks as an icon of sport. And McKinsey is generally acknowledged as an icon by anyone who has an understading of management consulting. If there is any disagreement about how iconic an organization is, then it is, by definition, not iconic.

Based on this definition, we selected 14 icons and researched what characteristics make them different from other organizations in their respective industries. What we found in essence is that all are able to maintain a virtuous circle of competence: by virtue of their leading status, they are able to attract and retain the best people. With the best people, they are able to form teams in which everyone is driven to get the best out of themselves; and with the best teams, they are able to strive for continuous improvement and adjustment of their results to maintain their iconic status (see *Figure 1-3*). Each of the iconic organizations we studied has, for at least half a century and under several successive leaders, been able to maintain the momentum of its success.

**Figure 1-3**   The Circle of Iconic Competence.

We shall return later in the book to take a more detailed look at how each section of the circle works, both within the RCO and in other iconic organizations. But first, let us give you a foretaste of the power of this circle, taking elBulli as an example.

## elBulli: A Recipe for Magic

Until its voluntary closure in 2011, elBulli was the gastronomic icon of the restaurant world (it is reinventing itself as a culinary thinktank and lab[16]). In 2002, 2006, 2007, 2008 and 2009, the restaurant was placed by *Restaurant Magazine* at the top of the list of the world's best restaurants, based on the opinions of 500 critics. Head chef Ferran Adrià appeared on the front pages of *Le Monde* and the *New York Times Magazine*, and half a million people competed against one another each year to secure one of the 8,000 seats at his dinner table. In short: it was a undisputed icon in its field.

Although it was Adrià's arrival at elBulli that heralded the beginnings of the restaurant's climb to the summit of world gastronomy, the seeds of this success were sown much earlier. The German homeopath Dr Hans Schilling opened the restaurant in 1964 besides his mini golf course. He had a keen interest in gastronomy and attracted chefs of an increasingly high standard. He himself introduced new ideas and unusual ingredients. Most importantly, he encouraged his people to visit the best restaurants of Europe and to learn from what they saw. Under the aegis of head chef Jean-Louis Neichel, who arrived in 1975, elBulli earned its first Michelin star. In the early eighties, the restaurant was taken over by business director Juli Soler and head chef Jean-Paul Vinay, who led the restaurant to its second Michelin star. Adrià began his career at elBulli with an internship in 1983, and became the new head chef in 1987.

Up until the year he became the new head chef, Adrià had mainly concerned himself with learning from and imitating other top restaurants. In that year, he attended a lecture by chef Jacques Maximin, who declared: "To create is not to copy." This became Adrià's new mantra, and it was

[16] See its manifest on elbullifoundation.com

this that enabled him in 1990 to regain the second Michelin star which elBulli had lost some years before. The coveted third Michelin star followed in 1997, and in the years that followed, elBulli grew to become the highest-rated restaurant in the world.

30 July 2011: the elBulli team prepares dinner for the last time. It chose to reinvent itself as a culinary thinktank

To reach these heights, Adrià had a formidable group of people at his disposal. Each year, elBulli received 4,000 applications from newly-qualified chefs. Of these, he selected 40 to start an internship. They travelled from all over the globe for the opportunity to work 12 hours a day, 6 days a week, in return for no more than board and lodging. The best of them (around 20 ) were invited to come back the following year, and the best of all were finally admitted to the group of seven *chefs de partie* for a salary of 1,500 euros a month, or about $1,720. The four head chefs who worked alongside Adrià had, almost without exception, started out as *chefs de partie*. In total, about 60 people worked in the restaurant each day, serving meals to 50 guests.

One of the most important ingredients of elBulli's philosophy was an unwavering respect for every team member, regardless of position or experience, and regardless of whether they were waiters or chefs – everyone was regarded as essential.[17] An internship at elBulli was first and foremost an incredible learning experience, and Adrià shared his recipes, methods and techniques without reservation. "The more people I share them with, the more people will use them," was his attitude. Lluís Garcia, one of the dining room managers, described the roles of the head chef and business manager as follows: "Ferran [Adrià] is brilliant, indefatigable and above all human. Juli [Soler] breathes life into elBulli and he is one of the people I admire most, because he knows how to create a team that is like a family."

With the help of this fantastic team, Adrià spent the six winter months that elBulli was closed each year developing a completely new and innovative menu. In his kitchen complex (or more accurately, laboratory), which covered an area of 325 square meters, around 50,000 experiments with food were carried out each year. Adrià personally tasted all successful experiments ("Don't give me anything that doesn't taste good"). About 500 experiments finally made it into the recipe books. Each recipe was stored in an enormous database, along with a rating of one, two or three stars. When the restaurant opened again, the team put together a menu of 35 dishes, which evolved day by day, partly based on feedback from guests.

---

[17] The information in this paragraph is mainly drawn from Prats, Quintanilla & Mitchell (2008).

Adrià's urge to innovate was huge: "Everything in elBulli must be renewed for the following year," he stipulated. "Every dish must be new. And it has to be good; the fact that we've never done it before is no excuse." Adrià was of the opinion that elBulli had in this way "developed more techniques and concepts in the previous fifteen years than the world in the past hundred". This produced dishes such as vanilla chips, perfectly spherical olives, blocks of curry with chicken sauce, or the mummy: a skeleton of fried red mullet with candyfloss.

This constant stream of innovative dishes, which Adrià spread around the world, once earned him the nickname of the "Salvador Dali of the Kitchen". Fellow head chef and former Adrià disciple Joan Roca described him as follows: "Ferran is a world leader. He influences everyone. I think that his most important contribution lies on a conceptual level. He teaches people that they must not feel limited by the past, and he obliges them to think and invent anew."

What is perhaps somewhat surprising, given its enormous popularity, is that the restaurant was loss-making – elBulli remained afloat with the help of side businesses, such as books and consulting. Adrià: "What would be the most logical thing to do? Raise the prices? A menu would end up costing 600 euros (or $690, instead of230 euros, or $265 )]. But I don't cook for millionaires. I cook for people with feeling."

# The Structure of this Book

elBulli shows how simple the circle of iconic competence essentially is: the most innovative food exerts an enormous attraction on the best people, from whom elBulli puts together a fantastic team, which can in turn produce even more innovative food. But if the circle is so simple, why then are there so few iconic organizations? It turns out that each of the three sections of the circle is more difficult to develop and sustain than perhaps at first appears. And even organizations that have been iconic for a long time and have a robust circle need to watch out that they don't slacken off in one of its parts. If they do, then it can mean a decline in iconicity, even though this usually appears to be temporary: the circle is usually so deeply embedded that it can still be picked up again.

The three main section of the circle of iconic competence – talent, team and time – form the backbone of this book. Chapters two to four list the necessary ingredients for each of these three sections, show how to maintain them and highlight what can put them at risk.

Chapter Two is about attracting and retaining the right people: talented people who are enthusiastic about what they do and have the right fit with the organization. The most difficult part is always maintaining the high standards. Even a small number of people who do not have the right profile can pull down a whole organization. This means that sometimes individuals have to be asked to leave, which is one of the hard tasks for managers of iconic organizations.

Chapter Three discusses what you need to forge individuals into a team in which everyone feels responsible for getting the most out of themselves. Of course, good leadership plays a very important role here. And this is where the danger also lies: the leader must never become bigger than the team, because this could signal the demise of the organization as a whole.

Chapter Four is about how to achieve outstanding results over time, through continuous adjustment and unwavering aspiration. Overconfidence and complacency are the human frailties which stand in the way of progress in this section: those who do well can easily think they can do everything, and that their success is a given. An organization that wants to remain an icon must avoid this.

Chapters Two to Four each contain in themselves three essential elements which we have consistently found in the iconic organisations that we studied. These three chapters describe a total of nine ingredients which form the *what* of the circle (see also *Figure 1-3*). The three chapters that follow discuss the *how* of the circle.

There seem to be a number of surprising similarities in the way in which iconic organisations maintain the circle of iconic competence. This is the subject of Chapter Five. For instance, the German idea of *Mitbestimmung* – literally "deciding things together" – appears to be an important principle for maintaining iconic status in the long term. It anchors the circle in the whole organization and makes it much less dependent on individuals.

Chapter Six addresses the question of how the circle can be set in motion, both in new and in existing organizations. Visionary leaders who surround themselves with a group of outstanding people appear to be present at the birth of most starting icons. But to maintain the virtuous circle once the leader has left the stage, it is important that good-quality DNA be incorporated early enough into the genes of the organization.

Chapter Seven is about icons of big industry. How do the most successful organizations become iconic in their main areas of competence? How do they ensure that their managers can continue to focus on results, and not be distracted by internal company politics? Can the circle of iconic competence also work in companies with tens of thousands of employees? We will attempt to answer these questions by using two examples: one of the biggest publicly listed companies in the world (Shell) and one of the best-performing conglomerates (Danaher).

Finally, in Chapter Eight, we discuss how iconic organizations can retain their significance in the information age, and how they can relate to open collaborative groups such as Wikipedia. We will show that these two organizational forms can both be important for different goals and how open collaborative groups can even strengthen iconic organizations.

Throughout the book, we provide as many examples as we can to illustrate our points. For the organizations that we use, we will focus mainly on the ingredients of the circle that are relevant to the chapter in question and not discuss every part of the circle for every organization. In all major examples of iconic organizations in this book (see *Figure 1-4)*, we can in fact identify each element of the circle of iconic competence. The fact that not every element can be found in the text for every organization is therefore a choice we made to improve readability, and not an inherent weakness of the organizations being used as examples.

Our ultimate goal is not to unravel the magic of a performance of Mahler, of a recipe of elBulli or of the game of the All Blacks. What we do aim to do is motivate people to create the same set of conditions and produce the same results as iconic organizations - "more of the extraordinary", as Dieter Flury, solo flautist and business director of the Vienna Philharmonic, describes it. Or, to use Jansons' metaphor, how can we become the ignition source for new three-stage rockets into space?

| Iconic Organization *in order of appearance in this book* | Iconic Competency | Year of Creation |
|---|---|---|
| Royal Concertgebouw Orchestra (RCO) | Symphonic classical music | 1888 |
| elBulli | Gastronomy | 1964 |
| McKinsey | Management consulting | 1926 |
| All Blacks | Rugby | 1905 |
| Steinway & Sons | Piano manufacturing | 1853 |
| W.L. Gore | Technology-driven product innovation | 1958 |
| Berlin Philharmonic | Symphonic classical music | 1882 |
| Vienna Philharmonic | Symphonic classical music | 1842 |
| Harlem Globetrotters | Basketball, entertainment | 1927 |
| Johns Hopkins Medicine | Hospital and medical University | 1889 |
| Shell | Oil and gas extraction | 1907 |
| Procter & Gamble | Innovation and marketing of consumer products | 1837 |
| Danaher | Acquisitions and performance improvement | 1969 |
| Institute for Advanced Study in Princeton | Fundamental scientific research | 1930 |

**Figure 1-4**   The organizations we studied which embody the Circle of Iconic Competence.

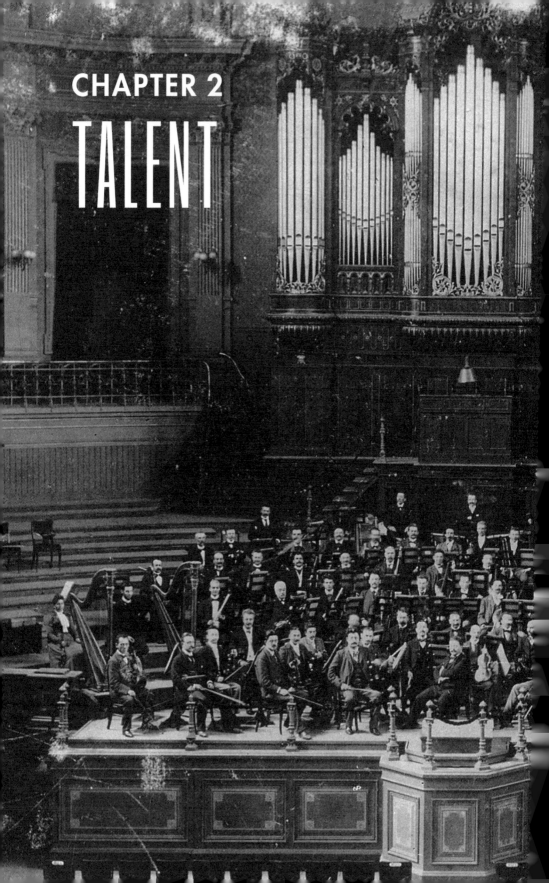

# CHAPTER 2
# TALENT

The Royal Concertgebouw
Orchestra in 1895 with
its new chief conductor
Willem Mengelberg

This chapter discusses
attracting and retaining
the right people: people
who have talent and
passion for their jobs and
have the right fit with the
organization. The most
treacherous aspect of this
process is maintaining the
highest standards. Even
a handful of people who
turn out to be less suitable
can bring down a whole
organization. To prevent
this from happening is
one of the most difficult
tasks for the managers of
iconic organizations.

# The Audition

'Ladies and gentlemen; Candidate Number One.'

From behind a screen, we hear the sound of shuffling. A music stand is being adjusted. The candidate decides to change position slightly. Now the tuning can begin; the pianist plays an 'A'; the clarinettist follows. The process is repeated – the sound is hesitant. Then the pianist begins to play an excerpt from Wolfgang Amadeus Mozart's clarinet concerto, and a few bars later, the candidate joins in. We still see nothing; everything is taking place behind a screen.

We are in the Recital Hall of the Amsterdam Concertgebouw and attending an audition. This is the musical equivalent of a job application, and every would-be member of the orchestra has to go through it. The first two rounds take place completely anonymously behind a screen, to exclude any kind of favouritism or unconscious bias. The only thing that counts is the quality of the candidate's performance.

The audition committee consists of orchestra members, with representatives from all musical sections (strings, woodwinds, brass, percussion). They listen attentively, read and move along with the music, and make notes on the forms they have to fill in. Some frown, then smile and yet others give a momentary look of understanding. But the mood is predominantly serious – the tension the candidates feel seems almost to infect the committee members. They have the important task of deciding who has achieved the absolute world-class standard in music that the Royal Concertgebouw Orchestra requires, and who is capable of producing a tonal quality that is in keeping with the orchestra. And, of course, they determine one of the most important career steps in the lives of the applicants.

Candidate Number One battles his way bravely through the Mozart. But (s)he has a lot of false *air*; in the quieter passages, the rasp of his breath all but drowns out the tone produced by the clarinet. The *dynamics* of the piece are good (it is loud and soft in the right places), and the *phrasing* is right (it is played with the correct musical syntax). But it lacks the velvety sound so typical of the RCO. In the lower notes, the clarinet seems to growl, in the higher reaches it almost squeaks. It's obvious that this candidate at least will not be receiving an invitation to go through to the second round.

"Dank u wel! Thank you!" the chair of the committee calls, once the candidate has played all three set pieces. More shuffling from behind the screen. A few minutes later: 'Ladies and gentlemen: Candidate Number Two'. And Candidate Number Two is clearly suffering from a bad case of nerves; you can hear the deep, shaky sighs between passages. After ten minutes of suffering, another "Dank u wel! Thank you!"

Candidate Number Three begins very promisingly, but in the Johannes Brahms sonata that follows the Mozart, the build-up to the crescendo seems to be missing – it all sounds a bit flat. Candidate Number Four is careless in the arpeggios. Candidate Number Five , on the other hand, sounds full of confidence – even when tuning up, you can hear that (s)he has the situation fully under control. (S)he seems to be enjoying it, and when you hear this candidate play, (s)he suddenly makes it sound very easy; never for a moment are you afraid (s)he will do something wrong. Could it be that (s)he will be allowed through to the next round?

We're running way behind schedule. After two and a half hours, only the first nine candidates have been heard. Time for a short break. Some committee members heave a small sigh of relief – a moment's relaxation, a pause in concentration and a stretch of the legs. Following that, there is another session that lasts deep into the evening.

The Royal Concertgebouw Orchestra in 2012 with its chief conductor Mariss Jansons

# Finding and Keeping the Right People

Just like all the other iconic organizations we have studied, the RCO devotes enormous amounts of time and effort to finding and keeping the right people, at every level. Why? The former chief conductor Mariss Jansons describes what makes an orchestra good in the first place: "Great players, certainly. And then an enormous drive to get to the right level; the pride to show high quality; and I think individuality and musical intelligence, which means that you can speak with musicians on a high level about your interpretations, and not just work on the primitive level. They must have a drive that never allows them to play below their level."[1]

Herbert von Karajan, the former chief conductor of the Berlin Philharmonic, once said: "The weakest player on the back row of the second violins determines the quality of the orchestra."[2] That's the crux of the matter. It's not about finding *a few* good people, with the idea that they will raise the rest up with them. No; *everyone* in the orchestra must belong to the absolute best in the world, because even if only a small number of people don't make the grade, they can still pull down the level of the whole orchestra.

Steve Jobs was quick to see this piece of wisdom, and applied it when recruiting the people who would build the first Macintosh in 1982. "What I saw in Woz (Steve Wozniak, his fellow founder of Apple) was somebody who was 50 times better than the average engineer. The Mac team was an attempt to build a whole team like that, A players. People said they wouldn't get along, they'd hate working with each other. But I realized that A players like to work with A players, they just didn't like working with C players ...you need to have a collaborative hiring process. When we hire someone, even if they're going to be in marketing, I will have them talk to the design folks and the engineers."

Jobs also saw the great danger that lies in lowering standards: "If you want to build a team of A-team players, you have to be ruthless. It's all too easy, if the team is growing, to add a couple of B-team players. Later, they will

---

[1]  D. Lister (2009). 'Maestro with a Mission'. *The Independent*, 8 April.

[2]  T. Grube (2008). *Trip to Asia – Die Suche nach dem Einklang*.
    Boomtown Media International.

attract C-team players." Jobs called the influx of B- and C-team players in the companies around him the *bozo explosion.*

Jobs always stuck to his mantra of only hiring the best of the best. This is what enabled Apple to develop, test and roll out the revolutionary OS X operating system with only 600 people within the space of two years. This operating system still forms the basis of current Apple computers. In comparison: Microsoft needed ten thousand people and five years to program Windows Vista, which subsequently was never seen as a great success.[3]

Later in this chapter, we will look in more detail at what exactly iconic organizations do to retain their A-players. But first, we will use the example set by McKinsey to illustrate how the important elements of this process can work in practice.

# The McKinsey Mystique[4]

McKinsey – or *The Firm*, as employees of the company like to call it – exerts an almost mythical sense of attraction on the business world's most ambitious graduates. The company is the number-one employer for people with an MBA from Harvard Business School, far ahead of Goldman Sachs in second.[5] On Vault, the influential career site, McKinsey has for ten years running headed the list of the most prestigious consultants to work for.

James O. McKinsey founded his company in 1926; right from the very start, his vision was to attract the best people to serve the most prestigious clients with the highest standards of professionalism. McKinsey was himself a professor at the University of Chicago, and six years after the founding of the company, he was able to join forces with Marvin Bower, a graduate of both Harvard Law School and Harvard Business School, who was working at a prestigious law firm. After a few tumultuous years – a failed merger, the sudden death of its founder McKinsey and an internal split – starting in 1939, Bower was to lay the foundations of the iconic organization we know today working from the newly independent New York office. (The Chicago office continued to operate as A.T. Kearney, a company that still provides consulting services to leading companies).[6]

McKinsey nowadays receives huge numbers of applications each year – many times more than there are vacancies. The selection process is among the most stringent in the industry. Why are so many of the world's brightest so keen to do a job which requires them to travel half the globe and often work more than 60 hours a week? The answer is simple: because they can learn there from the greatest concentration of the best people in industry. In the words of a consultant of the firm: "McKinsey forms a challenging environment where I am surrounded by people who value my development. In six months at McKinsey, I grew professionally more than I did in eight years at school and university."[7]

The first step in the selection process is to review the CVs. Not only is analytical ability taken into account (difficulty of study choice, good university, high grades and possibly a prestigious job), but also potential team, client and leadership skills (leadership positions while at university, teams managed and new initiatives launched). Those who are invited to interview go through a two or three-round process, each with a number of intensive *case interviews*. These are conducted by the consultants themselves. In these case interviews, abstract practical situations are presented to candidates to test their abilities to quickly structure and solve complex problems, and communicate their answers.

Little wonder, then, that candidates experience the process as highly competitive – it is not unknown for candidates to practise case interviews with people they know for months in advance, only to fall by the wayside in the first round. On Glassdoor.com, the site that compares employers based on anonymous input from employees, McKinsey tops the list of companies with the most difficult job interviews. However, it is interesting to note

[3] M. Mankins, A. Bird & J. Root (2013). 'Making Star Teams Out of Star Players'. *Harvard Business Review*, Jan – Feb 2013.

[4] Title taken from J.A. Byrne (1993). 'The McKinsey Mystique'. *BusinessWeek*, 19 September 1993

[5] http://www.hbs.edu/recruiting/alumni/employers.html, retrieved on 22 January 2013.

[6] J.W. Lorsch (2001). *McKinsey & Co*. HBS Case study.

[7] J. Minners (2011). 'A Decade of Dominance for McKinsey & Company in Vault Consulting Prestige Rankings'. Vault blogs, http://blogs.vault.com/blog/consult-this-consulting-careers-news-and-views/a-decade-of-dominance-for-mckinsey-company-in-vault-consulting-prestige-rankings, opgehaald op 17 maart 2013.

that despite the many rejections, 64% percent of candidates describe the process as "very positive", which is one of the highest scores; only 8% percent describe it as a "negative experience". A possible reason for this is that McKinsey generally gives clear and useful feedback as to why a candidate has been rejected, and for this reason most candidates experience the process and its final outcome as fair – even if it is negative.

After the final round, only the very best candidates receive an offer to join the firm, as testified by one business school professor: "McKinsey has not always recruited every very bright student I'd have liked them to have picked from my classes ... but, unlike their competitors, they have never picked one from my classes who isn't bright. I'm impressed by that."[8]

Even after the onboarding process, McKinsey remains committed to making sure its team consists only of A-players. An extensive internal training programme is an important part of this. Furthermore, McKinsey has, since the 1950s, applied its infamous *up-or-out principle*: those who do not get promoted within an allotted period are asked to leave. Around one in ten of the consultants who join McKinsey make it through to partner, and even here, the evaluation and selection continues unabated. "McKinsey spends an enormous amount of time and money on evaluations," says Robert Reibestein, former chair of the RCO Foundation and former senior partner at McKinsey and head of McKinsey EMEA.[9] "I spent several weeks a year evaluating the performance of senior partners on the other side of the Atlantic."

Surprisingly, the application of up-or-out itself causes little resentment among employees who are asked to leave. This is because evaluations are made based purely on quality, while the process is transparent and continuous feedback is given. For this reason, everyone knows at any given moment where they stand, and the signal to leave never actually comes

---

[8]  D. Newton (2001). 'Requirements for McKinsey Job'. *Businessweek forum*, http://forums.businessweek.com/discussions/BW_Business_Schools/Business_Schools_ War_Stories/Requirements_for_McKinsey_Job/bw-bschools/14745.3?redirCnt=1&nav =messages, accessed 4 April 2013

[9]  EMEA = Europe, Middle-East and Africa.

[10]  F. Naaijkens (2010). 'De loopbaan van LinkedIn-baas Eugenie van Wiechen'. *Intermediair*, 27 April.

unexpectedly – in most situations, employees avoid this by making an "anticipatory departure". Moreover, McKinsey will always help departing colleagues to find a good job – for the rest of their career. Former director of LinkedIn in the Netherlands, Eugenie van Wiechen, once described how she still continued to meet with her former mentor from McKinsey for lunch every six months, even though she had only worked there as a consultant for a short time.[10] Her mentor continued to help her, gave her career advice and, where necessary, helped her extend her network. Those who have once worked for *The Firm* remain forever part of the family.

The results of this approach speak for themselves. McKinsey is by far the biggest, best-known and most prestigious strategic management consulting firm. Although the company does not comment on its financial performance, annual turnover was assumed to be around $7 billion in 2010, with a total of 17,000 employees, 9,000 of whom were consultants. Finally, the company has an extensive alumni network that includes many top executives. The CEOs of Vodafone, Deutsche Post, Reed Eslevier, Boeing, BMW; the former CEOs Harvey Golub of American Express and Louis Gerstner of IBM; the COO of Facebook, Sheryl Sandberg – all members of the McKinsey family. It's not without reason that *Fortune* describes the company as "the best CEO launch pad".

## The Three Building Blocks of Attracting the Best Talent

When it comes to attracting top talent, the parallels between McKinsey and the Concertgebouw Orchestra are unmistakable. First, they both exploit their iconic status to make the pool of talent from which they fish as deep as possible. Second, they implement an extremely rigorous selection process which is aimed entirely at finding the most competent and suitable individuals. And third, everyone who has come through the selection process must continue to perform at the level the organization requires, so that the team consists exclusively of A-players. We see these same three elements in other iconic organizations (see *Figure 2-1*).

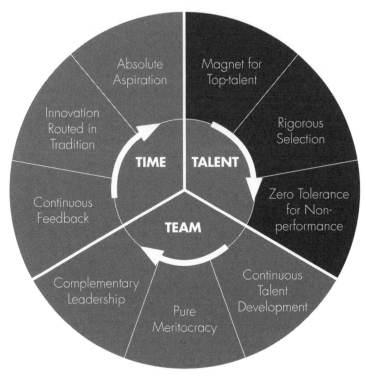

**Figuur 2-1**   The three elements of the Circle of Iconic Competence
for recruiting and retaining the right people.

In the following part we will explain each of the three elements of the
'Talent' section of the circle in more detail. In the closing part of the chapter, we will deal with how difficult it can be to keep the standards high and
to prevent B and C players from infiltrating the team.

## 1. Magnet for Top Talent

Iconic organizations use the power of attraction that their status brings to
retain top talent (in Chapter Six we will look at how organizations which
are not yet iconic can still recruit strong players). The reason for this power of attraction is simple: A-team players want to work with – and learn
from – other A-team players. We see this at Apple, we see it at McKinsey
and we also see it in the Concertgebouw Orchestra. "The musicians in the
orchestra are just amazing." This is the reason given by Julia Tom, orginally
Chinese American and former first solo cellist with the Berlin Philharmonic, for wanting to join the RCO.

Interestingly, salary considerations do not play a decisive role in deci-sion-making. At leading consulting firms Bain, BCG and McKinsey, sala-ries are in each case comparable. Apple pays its software developers at least 10% less than its competitor Google[11] – apparently the power of attraction is so great it compensates for the salary difference in the minds of the pro-grammers. And although the Concertgebouw Orchestra pays its musicians more than the other Dutch orchestras, it is not well known in the interna-tional music world for its high salaries; the salary of a leading player can sometimes only be half of what is usual in a top German orchestra.[12]

So the Concertgebouw Orchestra does not compete primarily on salary in its endeavour to attract top talent, but by other means. Besides the in-herent attraction exercised by international fame, the positive atmosphere among orchestra members is an important reason for musicians to want to play in the RCO. Tom: "In every other orchestra you will find people who regard music making as just another job. But nobody thinks like that here. Everyone in Amsterdam always wants to go for the best. At the same time, everyone understands that you can sometimes have an off-day. That can happen. But ultimately, we're all here to have fun making music, at the very highest level." A unique combination, therefore, of performance drive, a sense of perspective, and pleasure at work which exerts an irresistible power of attraction on the best musicians.

Moreover, the RCO doesn't just use its iconic status to attract the best orchestra members. "Winning first place in the *Gramophone* awards also helps us with our marketing and when negotiating our fees with con-cert halls," says Herman Rieken, percussionist and former chair of the Concertgebouw Association, of which almost all support staff and players are members. "In addition we have agreed a pay ceiling for guest conduc-tors. That is sometimes a challenge – after all, we need the best conductors in the world to keep our musicians inspired – but ultimately almost all top conductors want to stand in front of our orchestra, because they regard it as a pleasure to play with us, despite the lower fee."

[11] Glassdoor.com (2012). '15 Tech Companies' Software Engineer Salary Revealed'. *Glassdoor Report*, http://www.glassdoor.com/blog/15-tech-companies-software-engineer-salary-revealed-glassdoor-report, opgehaald op 24 January 2013.

[12] F. Don (2013). 'Orkestmusicus: geen gewone baan' (p. 141-155). In: M. Khalifa (red.). *Bravo! 125 jaar Het Concertgebouw en Koninklijk Concertgebouworkest*. Amsterdam: Uitgeverij Balans.

As well as playing on the inherent power of attraction that international fame brings, the orchestra also actively uses its unique atmosphere to recruit members. "If, after an audition, we fail to find anyone suitable, we sometimes invite top musicians to play a programme with us, so that they can experience how unique it is to make music in the Concertgebouw," says Rieken. Unlike the pure quality of the music, the unique culture of the orchestra is much less well known. Tom: "Before I joined the RCO, I had no idea the people were so amazing, only that they could play extremely well."

Other "soft" factors also play a role in attracting people to play with the orchestra. For example, the RCO can provide funds to allow its members to play on special and expensive instruments on long-term loan – a perk that goes back all the way to the very first years of the orchestra's existence.[13] Moreover, the orchestra has a very people-focused human resources policy, with ample opportunities for individual training and development. Finally, the chance to rehearse and play concerts with the world's best conductors in one of the world's best concert halls is, of course, a unique part of the RCO's proposition to top musicians.

The Orchestra Academy, set up in 2003, is an important initiative designed to attract more young top musicians. "Last year [in 2012] we took on 7 academicians out of 280 applications", says Jette Straub, who was in charge of the project at the time of the interview. "The academicians play an average of 10 to 12 programmes in the orchestra and, for each programme, are assigned a mentor who goes through the music with them and shows them the way in the orchestra. Our goal is to develop new orchestral musicians, and in doing so create a hotbed for the orchestral musicians of the future." Moreover, the academy builds a bridge between the academic training and professional orchestral practice, and plays thus a broader role in developing successful orchestral musicians.

However, the activities of the orchestra pale into insignificance besides the recruitment machines developed by some consulting firms and banks. "Even though an exciting career in Silicon Valley may appeal more to the

---

[13] J. Giskes (1989b). 'De Periode Willem Kes (1888-1895)' (p. 36). In: van Royen et al. (1989).

[14] I. van Heusden (2012). 'Animo om bankier te worden daalt al jaren in Amerika'. *NRC Weekend*, 9-10 Feb. 2013.

imagination, the financial services and consulting firms are still the biggest employers of Harvard graduates," writes the *NRC*.[14], a leading Dutch newspaper. An important reason is their slick recruitment procedures. Numerous information evenings and training sessions give potential applicants the greatest possible opportunity to speak to current employees in an informal setting. And, of course, the attractive pay and conditions also help. For the lucky ones, a contract can be waiting even before they have graduated, and it is not unusual for a bonus to be offered on signing to offset student loans. These companies clearly work very hard to increase their power of attraction to top talent.

## 2. Rigorous Selection

"It's a question of finding brilliant people who understand your dream," says lead bassist Dominic Seldis, paraphrasing the teachings of entrepreneur Richard Branson on how to find the right people. Solo trombonist and former chair of the artistic committee Jörgen van Rijen says of recruitment at the Concertgebouw Orchestra: "We look for people who are incredibly good *and* who want to fit into the whole. What's more, you have to be interesting as an individual in order to add something to the piece." The orchestra pours huge amounts of effort into finding people with this combination of qualities.

The process of recruiting musicians begins with an advertisement for an audition. In the past three years, there have been 21 auditions, attracting 1,753 applicants. Promising talents are invited to a first round which consists of playing a number of short pieces lasting four to five minutes from behind a screen. Those who are able to convince a majority of the audition committee go through to the second round, in which candidates are allowed to play a bit more, again from behind a screen. Musicians with extensive experience in top orchestras may start in the second round. For this round, too, those who gain a quorum of support from the committee go through to the last round, the 'final'.

In the final, candidates play for a total of about 25 minutes, and this time without the screen. Ultimately it is the committee, consisting of 20 to 25 members of the orchestra and the chief conductor – who has only one vote – that decides who, if anyone, is successful. Because a 60% majority is required, it often happens that no-one gets selected – in that case, a new audition is planned for the following year. Like the RCO, the Berlin Philharmonic is remarkably consistent in this: until someone of the right level is found, a position remains vacant and is filled by a temporary replacement when needed. In the last decade, one of the Berlin Philharmonic's two places for solo clarinet remained vacant for three years, for piccolo seven years and for solo horn as long as eight years.

Those who 'win' at the auditions (as the musicians call it) are given a trial period of a year, with evaluations after four and eight months, primarily to see whether they fit well into the orchestra. If necessary, the trial period can be extended for one and, theoretically, for two years. Twenty new members have succeeded in joining the orchestra in the past three years: barely more than 1% of the total number of applicants.

The parallels between the recruitment processes of top orchestras and those of leading consulting firms are remarkable. First, the selection is made based primarily on a direct competency test, an abbreviated version of the real work: concert excerpts in the case of the RCO and shortened case studies of real projects at McKinsey. Second, selection is made by people who do the work themselves and will therefore become future colleagues - the people in HR play only a supporting role. And third, the bar is set very high. Applicants must garner support from a clear majority of the selection committee, and few are ultimately chosen. In case of doubt, the committee prefers to take no one than to accept someone who is possibly not the A-player they are looking for and who could potentially pull down the quality of the organization. These three elements ensure that only the very best people join in, and that they show a good fit with the organization.

The rigorous recruitment process not only ensures that the right people are selected, but has the added advantage that talented young candidates who show great potential, but have as yet few qualifications, are still in with a serious chance. This is how Jaap van Zweden became concertmaster (the leader of the first violinists and second most important position in the orchestra after the conductor) with the RCO at the tender age of 19, and how a 21-year-old cellist and orchestra academician came along on the world tour organized in honour of the orchestra's 125th anniversary year at the insistence of the cello group. We see the same pattern at other iconic organizations: "It is noticeable how quickly players of potential can come through the All Blacks system if they are deemed to be All Blacks material", says journalist Spiros Zavos about the black-shirted New Zealand rugby team. "In this willingness to gamble on young talent the All Blacks selectors are rather like the selectors of the Australian cricket team in its glory days when boys from the bush were promoted and became great players because shrewd selectorial eyes saw greatness in them."[15]

The extreme pressure of the selection process in iconic teams is of course highly stressful for the candidates. Nearly all musicians dread the auditions that they have to go to: just a few minutes can make or break one's career. Added to this is the fact that anyone who wants to grow professionally and fill a different, better position in the RCO will have to take part in the auditions once more. Oboist Jan Kouwenhoven says that while in his regular position as second oboe, he often played solos on the cor anglais in the orchestra. "But I still had to audition for the regular position of the cor anglais. In the end, it wasn't me who got the job, but someone from outside the orchestra. That felt like a real blow at the time. But I learned to live with it, because the other person was at least as good as I was and because she was chosen as a result of an honest vote by the committee."

The other members of the orchestra endorse the enormous value of the extensive audition process. Trombonist van Rijen: "The fact that you know you have the support of the people around you is so important that it makes the cumbersome nature of the process worthwhile." Violinist Christian van Eggelen: "You feel enormously privileged if you win at the audition. That also forces you to prove you deserve that privilege, and to perform to the best of your ability time and time again."

## 3. Zero Tolerance for Non-performance

Once the candidates have made it through the selection process, they must then commit to perform at the level the iconic organization they have just joined requires. The Concertgebouw Orchestra, for example – contrary to many other orchestras – requires its musicians to commit to the job full time. Furthermore, the orchestra does not tolerate underperformance, although that process works in a very subtle way. "Everyone understands

---

[15] S. Zavos (2012). 'The next generation of All Blacks is coming forward'. *The Roar*, http://www.theroar.com.au/2012/05/14/the-next-generation-of-all-blacks-is-coming-forward, accessed on 28 January 2013.

that you can have the odd off-day, or even an off-week, and the rest of the orchestra will cover for you", says Van Rijen. "This constructive atmosphere is very important for the sound of the orchestra. But it does sometimes happen that someone underperforms consistently. In that case, the lead musician will discuss it with the artistic committee and suggest a plan of improvement. If that still doesn't work, then the orchestra member will be asked to leave. We all find that a real shame and, thankfully, it hardly ever happens."

Jan Willem Loot, who was Jan Raes' predecessor as general director of the RCO, stresses the importance of quality control: "Shortly after I started, I asked a number of poor performers to leave, both among the musicians and the support staff. It wasn't easy, and very much against the rules of Dutch culture, but in the end, everyone in the orchestra had developed such acute quality awareness that they all went along with it. In weaker orchestras, you can get away with a lot. If you see everyone giving a thumbs-up after every single solo, you know that there's something wrong; that just doesn't happen in top orchestras."

While quality control in the RCO is exercised in relatively subtle ways, in the Berlin Philharmonic the process is much more vigorous, especially in the case of candidates who are still in their probationary period. "There, the musician playing next to you is your biggest critic," says RCO first violinist Christian van Eggelen about the Berliner, where he has also played. All musicians start their time at the Berliner with a probationary period of two years, after which the whole orchestra votes on whether they are allowed to stay. "During the first two years, they really tested me to see how far they could bend me before I broke, just to see if I survived," says one of the orchestra members. "I really wanted to be one of them, but I had to understand that it just wasn't possible at that time."[16] Fergus McWilliam, who played first horn at the Berlin Philharmonic for 30 years and was until recently chair of the personnel committee, puts it like this: "Candidates must fight for their position, on the one hand by showing enough individuality, and on the other, by demonstrating the necessary flexibility and ability to adapt. They have to show clearly that they know when to lead, and when to follow."

[16] Grube (2008).

Whether they do so in a hard or a soft way, every iconic organization manages quality. The Cirque du Soleil, which in a few decades has grown from a group of street artists into by far the biggest circus group in the world, is no exception: "The performance evaluation system extends into every corner of the organization - both for artists and for support staff," says Hugo van Hulst, former production manager at Cirque. "Everyone was required to fill in an extensive self-evaluation. Your boss had to do the same, and you discussed the differences. That is in stark contrast to most other cultural organizations, where human resource policy is often seen as less important."

And yet it remains a difficult topic. "Ultimately, it's about people," says former RCO chief conductor Jansons. "You have to strike the right balance between striving for quality and keeping sight of the human side. I find it one of the most difficult parts of my job." Jansons tells an anecdote about fellow conductor Daniel Barenboim, who had to solve a sensitive situation at the Chicago Symphony Orchestra, an organization which, unlike Dutch orchestras, does not provide an automatic pension. "Barenboim asked a musician of advanced years, who was not playing like he used to, what his plans were for the future." The orchestra member answered: "I started out on this chair and I intend to finish on it." To which the conductor replied: "No problem, my friend. We'd be happy to carry the chair home for you."

## Never Lower Your Standards

Having to part ways with people who no longer make the grade is one of the reasons why it is difficult to keep the team of A-players you need to become and remain iconic. Another difficulty is the temptation to lower your standards in periods when it becomes hard to attract talent. For example, during the dotcom bubble at the end of the 1990s, many candidates who might otherwise have joined consulting firms went instead to internet companies. At the same time, the turnover rate of good people was very high. The consulting firms found themselves under great pressure to take on candidates who were not quite good enough, simply in order to meet demand. Those firms that succumbed to this temptation spent the next years dealing with the consequences. Within these companies, the

B players they had taken on risked becoming a slow-acting poison when the A players saw that they too could apparently get away with taking their foot off the gas. And so everyone lowered their standards. Even when the internet bubble burst, and talent was again thicker on the ground, these companies had to put a lot of time and effort into raising the bar back up to its old height.

Steinway, the piano builder founded in 1853, is a good example of a company that has always resisted the temptation to hire lower-quality people, even in times of rapidly-increasing demand (except, perhaps, when the company was under the ownership of media conglomerate CBS, which we shall deal with in Chapter Four ). In the selection process for Steinway employees, a great deal of attention is paid to conscientiousness and a sense of responsibility. Moreover, employees must be prepared to embark on an extremely long learning process. Given the craftsmanship of the work, it is more or less impossible to find people who, on joining the company, are already familiar with the specialized tasks of the production process. This means that they start with the simpler tasks and gradually work their way up to the more complex ones. Bruce Campbell, now intoner of the model D, the large concert piano, testifies: "Before I came to work here, I knew nothing about piano building. I first spent some time in tuning. And then I moved on to preparing the hammers for the intonation process.[17] After that I spent *ten years* intoning pianos, and doing more intoning, and yet more intoning. And only then did they think I might be ready for the real work on our best concert pianos."[18]

A refusal to make compromises when it comes to the demands placed on employees and the long learning process are both reasons why the production volume of Steinway grand pianos has remained relatively stable since 1860. In 1860, 1,800 grand pianos were built in the New York factory. In 2011, 2,000 were built, divided between New York and Hamburg.[19] In periods of higher demand, Steinway increased production only slightly. But the company was affected less badly in times when the market for pianos collapsed and when demand was limited to products of undisputable quality. This was crucial in making Steinway one of the few of the 1,400 piano makers that existed in 1910 to reach the 21st century.[20]

[17] In piano building, intonation is the process of adjusting the sound, for example by sanding the hammer heads to make them sound less woolly, or by pricking small holes in the felt of the hammer head so that they sound slightly less sharp. For every note, the hammer head must be intoned in just such a way that each tone has the same desired sound.

[18] B. Niles (2007). 'Note by Note. The making of Steinway L1037'. *Real Fiction.*

[19] To meet European demand, to avoid high import duties, and because one of the sons of Heinrich Steinway prefered to return to Germany, Steinway opened a second factory in Hamburg in 1880.

[20] A. Dolge (1911), *Pianos and their Makers*, Covina Publishing Company, p. 443 ff.

# CHAPTER 3

# TEAM

Before each game, the
All Blacks perform
their traditional Haka,
a Maori ritual

This chapter explores
the requirements for
merging talented
individuals into a team
in which everyone
feels responsible for
bringing out the
best in themselves. It
goes without saying
that leadership plays
a pivotal role here.
However, this also
harbours the greatest
danger: the leader
must never become
greater than the team,
as this might eventually
lead to the whole
organization's downfall.

# The Masterclass

It's 3 May 2012 and Mariss Jansons, together with the Royal Concert-gebouw Orchestra, is hosting a master class for three young conductors.[1] The British-Russian Alexander Prior is the youngest of them. Although he's only 19, he has already completed two master's degrees at the conservatory in Saint Petersburg, in composing and conducting, both with first-class honours. Moreover, he has composed dozens of works, and already conducted several professional orchestras. This is, however, the first time that he has stood in front of a world-renowned orchestra, with an audience, and under the critical eye of one of the world's most famous conductors.

The fifth part of *Symphonie Fantastique* by Berlioz lies open on the music stand. Prior picks up his baton, waits until everyone has their instruments at the ready, signals the orchestra to play, and … after a few notes, drops his baton, saying: "Very heavy, please, the same sound, but now twice as soft." He asks them to start playing again. The feedback from one of the viola players afterwards is harsh: "You've got a lot of self-confidence, but you need to contain yourself a bit. How can you interrupt a top orchestra after only the first few bars? If you do that with an orchestra that's not as nice as we are, they'll destroy you. And where will that leave you?"

A few minutes later, Prior asks the orchestra if they can play "with less inhibition". Jansons asks Prior what he means. "Umm … more forward." Questioning looks from Jansons. "Quicker!" A smile.

"Always be clear in saying what you want," Jansons advises. "Better still: *show* the orchestra what you want. If you want them to go faster, just wave your baton faster. If that doesn't work, you can always say it – but start by showing it."

The next day, Prior conducts the Concertgebouw Orchestra with his exuberant gestures through Shostakovich's Fifth Symphony. Jansons sets him the following exercise: "Just give them three beats, then stop conducting."

---

[1] This paragraph is based on an Avro TV documentary of the master class. Avro (2012). *Masterclass dirigeren: Mariss Jansons.* http://cultuurgids.avro.nl/front/detailklassiek. html?item=8277539, accessed on 5 April 2013.

The orchestra plays beautifully – Prior and Jansons don't need to do a thing; they just sit there smiling at each other.

Jansons: "The orchestra can play alone without a conductor. It's mysterious. So what's the use of the conductor? You have to make it a real performance, with your heart. You're one step ahead of everybody else; you know what you want to do. You lead them. A good orchestra doesn't need anybody to keep time. It needs inspiration. That's your job."

## From Top Talent to Top Team

An orchestra with a conductor is an almost perfect metaphor for a team with a leader. In a good team, everybody feels responsible for playing together in such a way that the whole thing operates in perfect harmony. The leader inspires everyone in the team to develop themselves, listens to what the team has to offer, and intervenes at just the right moments to make the whole more than the sum of its parts.

In this chapter, we discuss the second section of the circle of iconic competence: how to form a stellar team out of a group of fantastic individuals – which in itself already bears a tension. Highly-talented people typically know what they want and are very self-demanding. Equally high are their expections from the team they belong to.

In the Concertgebouw Orchestra, the team almost always adds an enormous amount to each individual's qualities. "In this orchestra, one plus one equals three," explains solo trombonist Jörgen van Rijen. The power of the RCO team lies for a large part in the enormous sense of responsibility that everybody feels for making the team a success. Each member of the orchestra expresses this sense of responsibility in their own way. Van Rijen: "Everybody is proud of the orchestra as a whole, and not of themselves." Lead bassist Dominic Seldis:"All the members really do care about the orchestra." Violinist Christian van Eggelen: "Everyone is enormously dedicated. You want to give your best on stage every evening. You see that same dedication in the management."

We do indeed see that same dedication in everyone, from the board members of the RCO Foundation right down to the stagehands. "I feel part of RCO history and one of the keepers of an icon," says Johan van Maaren, who takes care of logistics. He tells us about the tour to Armenia that he is planning: "We want to remain in control of the instruments at all times, so we are given special access at the airports. We travel with the instruments in the plane, and stay with them for the whole journey until they have arrived safely. Sometimes we work for 30 hours without a break. Of course, that's not really allowed, but nobody complains. The upside is that I'm completely free to manage my own time. There are three of us in the support team, and we really feel like we run our own business within the orchestra. And if we've helped make it a fantastic musical evening, then we feel really proud."

On the other hand, everyone takes it extremely personally when the team performance is below par. "Once, when we were in Vienna, the encore we did after the concert went completely wrong," recalls Seldis. "Even though it was only an encore, and the audience probably didn't even notice anything was amiss, the mood among the orchestra members was very somber, and everybody looked ashen. It was as if we'd had a death in the family. Everybody agreed: the RCO could do better than this, and we would never let it happen again."

A death in the family … we have heard those words before, coming from the mouth of an All Blacks player in describing the mood after a lost match. It shows the enormous sense of responsibility that can be witnessed again and again in the best teams. In the remainder of this chapter, we will look at the three elements that the Concertgebouw orchestra, the All Blacks and other organizations use to create teams with such a strong sense of responsibility.

But first, a short description of the All Blacks – a group of sportsmen with a sense of team spirit which, in its constituent parts, shows a striking number of similarities with that of the Concertgebouw Orchestra.

# Team Spirit at the All Blacks

The sport of rugby originated in England in the 19th century. The story goes that the sport began in 1823 when a certain William Webb Ellis, while playing a game of football at his school in the town of Rugby, suddenly picked up the ball and ran across the goal line. In the decades that followed, the sport of rugby was developed, and today has millions of followers worldwide. The sport demands an enormous amount of team coordination, because a single player who breaks through the line has almost no chance of scoring - his teammates cannot throw him the ball (because the ball can only be thrown backwards) and if he has the ball in his possession, he will almost certainly be tackled immediately by an opponent. A successful breakthrough in rugby, therefore, depends on the coordination of a number of players in combination, who act in a constantly changing formation.

At the end of the 19th century, rugby was successfully introduced into New Zealand, where it grew into a national sport. In 1905, the New Zealand team first played under the nickname the All Blacks, and began its impressive rise. Just as a reminder: the All Blacks have won 75% of all the matches they have ever played, gained on average twice as many points as their opponents, have been the number-one team in the world for longer than all other countries put together, and have a positive winning ratio against every country they have ever played against. Now that's an icon.

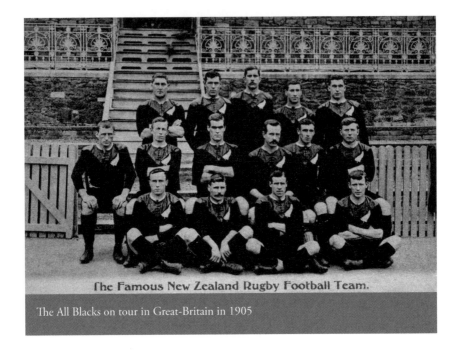

The Famous New Zealand Rugby Football Team.

The All Blacks on tour in Great-Britain in 1905

The All Blacks' team spirit is legendary. The players themselves say that team spirit adds another 30% to their performance.[2] At least ten books have been written about the processes and leaders that make this unique team dynamic possible, including a PhD thesis.[3]

*The legacy is more intimidating than any opposition.* This statement, made famous by All Blacks captain Richie McCaw, summarises the essence of the circle of iconic competence of the team. Legacy is synonymous with tradition, and *tradition* is the word that most members of the Concertgebouw Orchestra use to describe this feeling (though without any connotations of conservatism).

The towering tradition of the All Blacks is the reason why being asked to become a player brings with it such a huge burden. "The biggest feeling on earth really," said one player. Another: "It was the greatest thing that ever happened to me." That feeling alone makes the players want to give everything for their team: "I thought about the guys who had played in the No. 7 jersey before me and they were all my heroes," said a former captain. "And here I was. I didn't want to let them down. That was the most important thing for me; that I didn't want to let my number or my team down."[4]

This sense of responsibility drives a powerful combination of ambition and humility. John Bull, the founder of a small leadership consulting firm, wrote after speaking to a number of team members: "There is a strange characteristic of many All Blacks you meet - despite their profile as world-class performers, they tend to be incredibly humble and dismissive of their individual achievements. This is a common trait in other high-performing team environments and it seems to be a reflection of the total focus on team performance and the commitment of individuals to do whatever they can in the service of a cause they feel is much greater than them. Yes, every individual is focused on performing to the best of their ability, and they receive coaching and feedback to help them excel as individuals; but the motivation is service to the team, not individual glory.

One recent example of this is the way with which Ma'a Nonu has embraced the responsibility he was given to mentor Sunny Bill Williams, an up-and-coming player who may put his own position in the team at risk. Yes, Nonu is still very keen to play for the team, but he has poured all his experience into helping Williams play to his full potential; and the two 'rivals' are best of friends."[5] Developing young players is thus more important than individual glory.

For the All Blacks, development and innovation are more important than the avoidance of mistakes. In 2007, after the team had failed for the fifth time in a row to win the world championship, there were calls from many sides for both coach Sir Graham Henry and captain Richie McCaw to resign. However, they received the support of the team and the New Zealand Rugby Association, which allowed them to stay, and used that as an opportunity to up their game, and to learn from their mistakes. In 2011 and in 2015, the All Blacks won back the world cup.

[2]  Bull (2012).

[3]  T.W. Johnson (2012). A *case study of the winning ethos and organisational culture of the All Blacks (1950-2010)*. Palmerston North, New Zealand: Massey University (dissertation).

[4]  Johnson (2012).

[5]  Bull (2012) *Leadership insights from the performance environment of the All Blacks*. http://www.talltree.org.uk/articles/the-all-blacks.html#sthash.4lWucUkF.dpuf accessed 19 May 2014.

The emphasis on training and subordination to the team also applies to the team leaders. Sports journalist Alex Veysey wrote of a former player and leader of the team: "The side to [Colin] Meads' greatness, which many perhaps do not quite appreciate, is the contribution he makes in a side's corporate welfare. Colin Meads is a humble man, a man of action rather than a talker about his actions, yet he is always the unofficial adviser, guide, assistant, leader of any All Blacks party outside the official leaders of the side . . . Meads does not seek this position, the rest of the team simply place him in it."[6]

The informal leadership of the All Blacks has a long history, and is characterized by the "back seat of the bus". That was where the players who were regarded and accepted by the rest of the team as the leaders sat. Players had to earn a place on the back seat, based on their quality of play, team contribution and leadership. Often they were the more experienced players, but younger players could make it to the back seat, if they truly earned it. There was not just one leader with absolute power, but a group of people among whom power was distributed: the coaches, the captain, the back row of the bus.

This so-called collective, or distributed leadership, has in the last ten years become institutionalized and formalized by coach Sir Graham Henry. During team selection, care is taken to ensure there will be enough players with leadership quality in the team. One of the coaches: "So I think if you looked at one thing since 2004 that has been hugely influential in the All Blacks having a 86% or 87% winning ratio … it's the leader."[7]

# The Three Building Blocks of a Top Team

Just like the first section of the circle (discussed in Chapter Two ), here, too, we find three elements that are important to the RCO, the All Blacks and our other examples: continuous talent development, pure meritocracy (literally 'power by merit') and complementary leadership (see *Figure 3-1*).

[6] A. Veysey (1974). *Colin Meads All Black*. Auckland, New-Zeeland: William Collins.
[7] Johnson et al. *Collective Leadership: A Case Study of the All Blacks*. Asia-Pacific Management and Business Application, 1, 1 (2012).

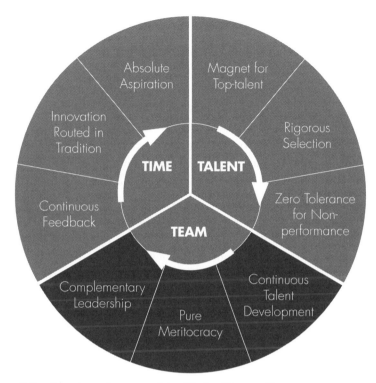

**Figure 3-1**   The three elements of the Circle of Iconic Competence for creating the best team.

Complementary leadership is the most important part of these three elements, and perhaps of the whole circle – the right leadership role is essential for every iconic organization. For this reason, we shall spend most time in this chapter on the question of how a good leader (just like a good conductor) ensures that he gets the best out of this team – and therefore really is complementary to the group. This theme runs through the entire chapter.

## 1. Continuous Talent Development

Iconic organizations offer talented people the greatest opportunities to develop themselves, because that is where they find the best people to learn from and the greatest challenges, allowing them to perform at the highest level. Robert Reibestein describes it as an essential part of the virtuous circle that has been in use at McKinsey for 80 years: "One: attract the best and the cleverest candidates. Two: develop, stimulate and support them, based on the McKinsey values. Three: place them in situations with the most demanding clients and the most complex business problems. Four: exceed client expectations and use that to build a very strong client portfolio, which will help with point one." Surrounded by the best of the best, talented people are thus challenged to perform to the utmost of their abilities and to develop themselves further in ever-more demanding situations.

Besides leveraging the intrinsic opportunities that iconic organizations have to offer, good leaders are also constantly on the lookout for opportunities to place their team members in challenging learning situations, and to motivate them to continue to get the best out of themselves. Interestingly, extrinsic motivators take a clear second place in these sorts of environments. If, for example, you have an important task for an employee to complete, then you tempt them with a reward, for example a bonus. The more important the task, the bigger the bonus, the more the employee does their best, and the sooner the job is finished ... or is it? Of course it is not. In his book *Drive*, Daniel Pink draws on volumes of scientific research to question in great detail the preconceptions that exist about where people find motivation.[8]

One of the most surprising pieces of research that Pink cites is a scientific study carried out, among others, by Dan Ariely, former professor at the renowned Massachusetts Institute of Technology (MIT) in Boston, and paid for by the US Federal Reserve.[9] In order to measure the effect of large monetary rewards on performance, the researchers traveled to rural India because, for relatively little money there, they could offer rewards of enormous value – 10 dollars being the equivalent of a month's salary. The experiment consisted of ten tasks, with participants being divided into three groups, each offered different levels of rewards for completing the tasks successfully: 50 cents, 5 dollars and 50 dollars (almost half a year's salary). What did they learn? The group working for 50 dollars performed statistically worse than the other two groups: in eight out of the nine tasks, *higher* reward led to *lower* performance.

It seems that extrinsic reward causes people to lose a large amount of their intrinsic motivation. This is especially true of creative tasks: high rewards put people under pressure, which means they can no longer think freely, but instead try to work shortsightedly towards a solution. This may work for repetitive tasks, but for creative work, this kind of myopic thinking and acting has the opposite effect.

It comes as no surprise, then, that money plays little or no role in motivating members of the RCO orchestra: pay differentials there are small. The soloists do earn a bit more than the tutti players, and they are not required to play as many concerts, but on the other hand they also bear more responsibility, are more easily heard by the audience, and often must practise more for their solo pieces. What is however important for the relationships in the orchestra is that all salaries are completely standardized and that no exceptions are made, even if that means that a top player ends up being poached by another orchestra (which, incidentally, almost never happens).

The importance of this strict pay policy is demonstrated by practices in orchestras in the United States. "In the US, pay differentials are often greater than in the Netherlands," van Rijen says. "On top of that, players who are doing well will start negotiating through their agent for a raise. In the Netherlands that would be out of the question. The pay gaps that then arise create tensions between colleagues and undermine motivation, the atmosphere in the orchestra, and ultimately the quality of the music." In conditions like these, team spirit flies out the window.

A healthy group dynamic is nevertheless crucial to creating an environment in which everyone wants and dares to perform. This emerged very clearly from our interviews with the musicians of the RCO. "Everyone in the orchestra is trusted to go for a perfect 10," says van Rijen. That means you run the risk that you sometimes get a six, and that's OK. In many orchestras people simply don't dare to take that risk, so they place a safe bet on a seven or eight." And players who go for a seven or an eight will rarely succeed in creating a night of magic in the concert hall. The level of trust within the orchestra is therefore an essential part of achieving greater levels of perfection.

---

[8]   D.H. Pink (2009). *Drive: The Surprising Truth About What Motivates Us.* New York: Riverhead Books.

[9]   D. Ariely, U. Gneezy, G. Loewenstein & N. Mazar (2005). *Large stakes and big mistakes.* Working paper series, Federal Reserve Bank of Boston, No. 05-11, http://hdl.handle.net/10419/55603. Pink explains this experiment in great detail and in an entertaining way in the YouTube video: http://www.youtube.com/watch?v=u6XAPnuFjJc.

It is also the case that achieving a perfect 10 is incredibly motivating. The orchestra members even call it addictive. This 'addiction' is the reason why the musicians continue to find their job stimulating, even though they often have to work hard for pay that is good but not great and for chances of promotion that are small - especially compared with a job in industry. "I feel valued, and feel part of an enormous tradition that I can build on," says the newly-appointed first violinist Marc Daniel van Beimen. Almost all the orchestra members use similar words to express why the orchestra continues to have a hold over them. The vast majority of orchestra members remain in service for a period of many years, most of them until their retirement at 65, and after that many continue to play regularly as replacements.

Stimulating the musicians' sense of intrinsic motivation is one way to foster the continuous development of talent in the Concertgebouw Orchestra. Providing training opportunities is another. For example, the orchestra offers its musicians the opportunity to take instrument lessons and master classes, anywhere in the world. And there is also scope for other training. Sports psychologist Rico Schuijers, who accompanied the Dutch Olympic team to London in 2012, gives lectures to the orchestra members on thinking skills, communication and group dynamics, followed by workshops and, if desired, individual sessions. The orchestra members can also suggest training sessions, such as relaxation techniques or career guidance. The only condition is that there has to be a real link to their work as musicians.

Training is not only about learning, for teaching is also encouraged. Members of the Concertgebouw Orchestra regularly give master classes to talented young musicians across the whole world. Some orchestra members find it incredibly stimulating to pass on their knowledge and skills to young musicians, and even regard this as an extra source of inspiration. Moreover, teaching is a way for them to continuously improve their own skills, and become conscious of things that they otherwise do automatically. And if they are training people who may later decide to become professional musicians, then that is an added bonus.

Of particular interest is how hierarchy is used as a way to develop talent. Each instrument section has its own different levels. With each successive level, the complexity of the music to be played increases. It is only logical that orchestra members grow and progress as they move up through this hierarchy. But what is surprising is that the *higher* they climb, the more *free time* they get. They are expected to devote this free time to activities that allow them to develop further as a musician, but in alternative ways. Often this will be in the form of teaching, but it can also be in the form of playing chamber music.

In the same way that learning and teaching are paths to personal growth, so chamber music stimulates both individual and collective development. Chamber music is performed by smaller groups and allows each musician to play a more prominent role. They learn to deal with nerves more effectively, are compelled to listen to each other better and build a deeper level of trust. There is no conductor, only an ever-changing game of leading (playing the main melody) and following (playing the accompaniment).

At the Concertgebouw Orchestra – and also in the Berlin Philharmonic – the playing of chamber music is greatly encouraged. For instance, the RCO gives an annual incentive award to young members of the orchestra who develop themselves further in the field of chamber music. At the Berlin Philharmonic, there are as many as 30 active chamber music ensembles. Because the members of the orchestra are so used to accompanying each other and trusting each other, these top orchestras develop the agility and dynamics of a string quartet.

Ultimately it is in the orchestra itself that the musicians can develop and express themselves the most. A story told by musical editor Thiemo Wind about former RCO solo horn player Jasper de Waal illustrates the enormous sense of team spirit and intrinsic motivation very well: "De Waal told me that he found it much more exciting to play a solo passage *in* the orchestra than to play a complete horn concerto solo *in front of* the orchestra. When he played a solo concert, he was accountable only to himself if something went wrong. But with a solo piece in the orchestra, he felt he was responsible to all the players in the orchestra."

We shall deal with this notion of responsibility in more detail later when we talk about complementary leadership. But first let us describe an important precondition for the sustained development of talent: meritocracy.

## 2. Pure Meritocracy

Meritocracy literally means 'power by merit'. The idea behind it is that those who perform the best get the biggest rewards and occupy the most important positions. That sounds like a principle of logic, but in many organizations the reality is different. Often the biggest rewards and privileges go to those who shout the loudest, have the most influential friends or play the smartest political game. This means that it is not always the most competent people who climb the corporate ladder, and organizations where this happens will never succeed in becoming iconic. To make matters worse, those who *are* competent will be less motivated to get the best out of themselves – after all, good work is not valued. "Meritocracy is very important for organizational success," says former Shell CEO Jeroen van der Veer. "It allows you to prevent tribal warfare, and is good for diversity. As a leader, you have to keep on working at it from the top down." In iconic organizations, meritocracy generates the trust that is needed from talented individuals to keep working on their development.

In the Concertgebouw Orchestra, meritocracy is so deeply ingrained that most orchestra members hardly even seem to notice it. The high value accorded to competence begins, of course, at the first audition, which is conducted from behind a screen. After that, promotion is only possible following a new audition process; this means that promotion is based fundamentally on musical quality. But even informally, value is placed purely on a person's level of musical ability. Seldis: "If you succeed in making a beautiful job of that arpeggio during the concert, and you see the smile on Jansons' face. That's a magical feeling."

The high value accorded to beautiful music is also the reason why being a loudmouth is completely frowned upon, regardless of the position a person holds in the orchestra. "A big difference with other orchestras is that in the RCO there are no superstars or *prima donnas*," says Seldis. "Anyone who tries to become one will be quickly reined in by the rest of the orchestra." First, they will do it with a joke or an ironic comment. But anyone who really does develop airs and graces will – so the story goes – receive a pep talk from one of the stagehands, who will tell them in the plain speech of Amsterdam that this really is not the way that members of the RCO are expected to behave towards each other. Even those who have not yet perfected their Dutch seem to have little difficulty in understanding what is meant.

The experienced orchestra members also play an important role in preventing prima donna behaviour. Robert Waterman, who has been lead violinist in the orchestra for almost 40 years and whose father, wife, brother and son were also connected to the orchestra ("my brother and I were a bit like those two old guys on the *Muppet Show*"), says that younger lead instrumentalists who had not yet developed a feel for the relationships in the orchestra were sometimes pulled up for this. "As a newcomer to the orchestra you need to understand that there is a lot of experience in the orchestra which you can and must use, even if you are a lead instrumentalist. We've sometimes exchanged harsh words about this, but always for the love of music and of the orchestra, and with mutual respect."

Waterman tells us more about the orchestra's meritocracy: "Suggestions as to how the music should be played are always judged on their merits, whether the idea comes from an acclaimed conductor or from someone on the back row. The orchestra can respond very enthusiastically to an interesting idea, and often develops it much further. Some conductors can find it hard to accept that anyone in the orchestra can just come up with an idea or ask a question. Our former chief-conductor, Riccardo Chailly, even made a rule that said the hierarchy could not be bypassed, and that if anyone had anything to say, they should do it through their section leader, who would bring the point to his attention. But this rule did not fit with the RCO at all, and was later scrapped."

The best consulting bureaus have a similar openness to good ideas. "McKinsey had a culture that fostered rigorous debate over the right answer without that debate resulting in personal criticism," says the experienced McKinsey man and former CEO of IBM Lou Gerstner in an interview with *BusinessWeek*. "It was the supremacy of the idea that was important, whether it came from the youngest associate or the most senior partner. The task was to come up with the right answer."[10]

---

[10]  Byrne (1993).

## 3. Complementary Leadership

"Maintain the upper hand without being authoritarian." That's how Waterman describes the paradoxical combination of qualities a good conductor needs. Thiemo Wind describes Jansons with these words: "humane, warm, demanding and funny." Successful conductors have, on the face of it, a paradoxical combination of personality traits.

The interesting thing is that successful leaders in the business world are also characterized by similar contradictions. Jim Collins, who spent many years studying successful companies, wrote of their leaders that they "are somewhat self-effacing individuals who deflect adulation, yet who have an almost stoic resolve to do absolutely whatever it takes to make the company great, channeling their ego needs away from themselves and into the larger goal of building a great company. It's not that Level 5 leaders have no ego or self-interest. Indeed, they are incredibly ambitious—but their ambition is first and foremost for the institution and its greatness, not for themselves".[11] In summary, he describes these kinds of leaders as displaying "a paradoxical blend of personal humility ('I never stopped trying to become qualified for the job') and professional will".

Being ambitious for one's team and not for oneself is encapsulated brilliantly in this quote by Larry Fink, one of the founders and also CEO of the BlackRock investment fund: "It will be a great moment for me when I see the firm doing better without me than with me. That's the difference between being a founder and being a CEO."[12] Good leaders feel like founders.

We can summarize all these characterizations under the term *complementary leadership*. The essence is that the leader makes their own interests subordinate to those of the team, takes the existing qualities as a starting point, and adds to them – the leader is complementary to their team. This complementary leadership is contained in the lessons that Jansons teaches his masterclass students at the beginning of this chapter, and we see it reflected consistently in iconic organizations.

The other phenomenon that we see time and time again in the organizations we have studied is *distributed leadership*. In other words, there is not one single strong leader in an organization, but power and responsibilities are divided over diverse leadership roles or even across all members of the team. This applies both formally (the coach and the captain of the All

Blacks) and informally (the 'back seat of the bus'). True distributed leadership means ultimately that anyone in the organization can act as leader, if that is necessary for the success of the team.

With the All Blacks, for example, the management once made the mistake of reserving a training pitch that was far too small. When the team members arrived, they stood around wondering what to do. Then Mils Muliaina, one of the players, said: "No problem, folks, we can do this – we just all need to play a bit smaller. Let's make this a fantastic training session." Where many other teams would have chosen a scapegoat and suffered a wasted afternoon, the All Blacks had a fantastic session.[13]

In the same way, a McKinsey consultant who has been with the firm for 18 months feels responsible for the quality of an analysis produced by a younger colleague who only has nine months under his belt. He will also not hesitate to instruct a manager who joins the team in the methodology that is to be followed. Distributed leadership is therefore closely related to complementary leadership: only complementary leaders can create the conditions in which distributed leadership can arise and flourish.

The lessons learned about leadership in orchestras can be directly applied in the business world – just replace 'conductor' with 'manager', and 'orchestra' with 'team'. The analogy between these two is so strong that some companies even send their managers for an afternoon of training in how to be a conductor, so they can learn at first hand how, using as few words as possible, you can lead a group of 120 people and get them to play together. In the history of the Concertgebouw Orchestra, the chief conductors have always played an important role. What is immediately striking is how long some of them have remained director of music of the orchestra. Willem Mengelberg, for instance, remained in his post for half a century, from 1895 to 1945. In the 125 years since its founding, the RCO has only had six chief conductors.[14] The average length of their chief-conductorship, 21 years, is almost twice the average in the top orchestras we analysed (see *Figure 3-2*).

[11] Collins (2001).

[12] H. Sender & D. McCrum (2012). 'BlackRock: Ahead of the Street'. *Financial Times*, 28 November.

[13] Bull (2012).

[14] In 2016, Daniele Gatti will become the 7th chief conductor of the RCO.

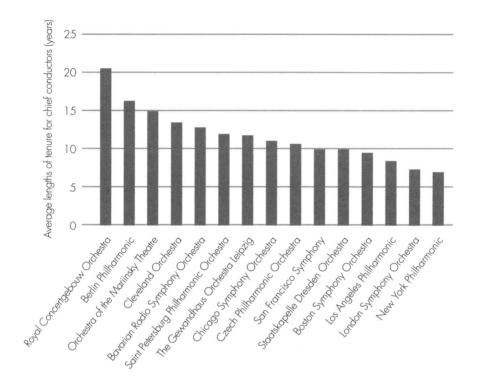

**Figure 3-2**   Average length of tenure for chief conductors at 20 leading orchestras of the world.[15]

Why is the chief conductor so important? What is his role? "Jansons' most important role is to give inspiration, trust and musicality," says Seldis. "Every evening, on the podium, you see Jansons die a little. You see it in his complexion and in his physical stature. The fact that he is willing to give that much is the reason why everyone in the orchestra wants to give their best." Jansons is a general who leads his troops from the front.

This is what Jansons himself says about his style of leadership: "I don't always know if I can manage it, but I can at least tell you what I try to do. I was always a perfectionist. My teachers were perfectionists - my father (the conductor Arvid Jansons), Mravinsky, Swarowsky and Karajan. But with the years I also began to ask myself: what makes a great performance?

Well, you can do everything fine. You can prepare right. You can get the texture as it is written in the score. Everything is on time. Ensemble playing is fine. Even the sound. But there is something else that is on a higher level. I call it the cosmic level. For me, notes are signs, like words, that convey associations. So the question is, what is behind the notes? What is the meaning and the atmosphere of the notes? This is the inner world of music, and if you can enter this world, this takes the performance on to a much higher level.

A conductor can achieve this through inner energy, or with the hands, or sometimes with words. It is easy to tell an orchestra to play a crescendo or an accent, but if you can create the right image, content and atmosphere, then they will play in a completely different and more meaningful way."[16]

Even Herbert von Karajan, a conductor with a reputation of being authoritarian, understood very well that he had to be complementary to the orchestra to make it play at its best. "The Berlin Philharmonic plays like one huge chamber music ensemble which constantly listens to itself, and whose leadership constantly changes," says Fergus McWilliam. "Von Karajan's secret was that he played into this constantly changing leadership, and made it more transparent. He knew when to lead and when to leave us to play."

The subtlety with which complementary leadership can be used to create magic is also apparent from the following anecdote related by Jan Kouwenhoven about the RCO: "We are a very sensitive orchestra. Chailly once said we are a mirror to the conductor. If a conductor has got something to offer, he immediately gets a lot in return. It's not about a perfect wave of the baton or anything like that. In fact, we're allergic to conductors who stand there looking at their own movements. For us, it's about personality. Take someone like Kurt Sanderling – he was an unusual kind

---

[15] Orchestra websites and H. Ferwerda (2013). 'Een uniek orkest' (p. 123-137). In: Khalifa (2013). The selection of orchestras is based on Gramophone magazine's top-20 by vote, but excludes those orchestras which, for long periods, have not had a chief conductor (Vienna Philharmonic and Metropolitan Opera Orchestra), and orchestras which were formed very recently (Saito Kinen Orchestra, Budapest Festival Orchestra and the Russian National Orchestra – all founded in the 1980s).

[16] M. Kettle (2004). 'Prime time'. The Guardian, 30 January.

of guy, and he conducted like he was washing windows, but he had an aura about him. I remember playing Bruckner's Fourth with him. The piece begins with a tremolo, very quietly. Sanderling told us to play softer, softer, and then exclaimed: 'like the rustling of trees in the forest!' That worked brilliantly. The third musical theme is much more upbeat, a bit like a dance, and then he suddenly shouts: *And here comes Bambi!* It's difficult to explain, but you really go the whole way for a man like that. Nobody plays safe; you dare to take risks. And then you get one of those rare moments where the orchestra really rises above itself."[17]

All this sounds very nice, maybe even a bit soft. But good conductors work very hard. Jansons is known for his enormous love of hard work and his sense of drive to carry on until he gets things right. "Jansons gives it all he's got – and he can't do any less," says cellist Julia Tom. "We once had an evening rehearsal of Mahler's Third. The next morning at 10 o'clock we had another rehearsal, and in Jansons' score of hundreds of pages he had noted down everything he wanted to change. He had spent most of the night preparing the rehearsal."

Jansons demands the same level of commitment from his team as from himself. "He can also be very strict," remarks stagehand Johan van Maaren about the rehearsals he sometimes attends. "He sometimes repeats a passage endlessly, until he gets it just the way he wants it."

Inspiration, ambition, sensitivity, a love of hard work. All important qualities in a leader. But when it comes down to it, complementary leadership begins with qualities that people already possess. "An orchestra is like a plane," German conductor Christian Thielemann once said. "You can steer it any way you want, but you have to bear in mind the intrinsic dynamics of the aircraft."[18] Jansons understands this better than anyone. "I don't want to change for change's sake. The change comes about naturally. Even in Oslo, my first post as chief conductor, I started by doing my job as best I could, and we grew together from there. If you impose your will on the orchestra, it's just an expression of your own oversized ego."

[17] Kurt Sanderling's words date from 1991; he died in 2011.
[18] Quoted by Dieter Flury of the Vienna Philharmonic in conversation with the authors.

Jansons told us this from his Amsterdam hotel room, a bowl of the most delicious chocolates on the table, an abundantly decorated fake Japanese Christmas tree in the background. We are fascinated by his insights into leadership, and we hope the words in this section give an impression of his vision – although we could continue for many pages on the leadership qualities of conductors. To learn more, we recommend the TED film *Itay Talgam: Lead like the Great Conductors*, or one of the YouTube videos about Leonard Bernstein's skills as a conductor – for example the performance of Haydn's Symphony no. 88, which he conducts only with his eyes.

Just as we are writing these words, Robert Waterman unexpectedly calls – the violinist with 40 years experience. "I just realized I forgot to say something important during our interview: the importance of the management. We talked the whole time about the conductors, but the management team members are also very important for the RCO. The same applies to them as to conductors. They need to make sure that they continue to listen to the members of the orchestra; that's something the current management team is very good at, by the way. I just wanted to say that."

## The Curse of Power

The danger for successful leaders of iconic organizations is that they can grow bigger than the organization itself, with the risk that iconic status cannot be conferred onto a new leader. Shakespeare understood like no other the potentially destructive nature of power. His classic *Macbeth* shows how someone with great leadership potential can go off the rails in the wrong set of circumstances.

Macbeth is ambitious, proactive, communicative and results-focused. He wants desperately to be loyal to his boss and to do the right thing for his organization. And he is loyal: "The service and the loyalty I owe in doing it pays itself," he swears to King Duncan. "Your highness' part is to receive our duties, and our duties are to your throne and state children and servants." In short, Macbeth is the perfect officer in the army of the king, and he gains quick promotion. After he successfully averts a major attack by the Norwegians, King Duncan makes him his right-hand man.

For a short while, Macbeth is pleased with his promotion, but he knows that he has more up his sleeve – especially now that he has been told by the witches that it is his destiny to become king. His wife manages to convince him how easy it will be to murder the present king in his sleep, now that he is a guest in his house. A quick stab in the back, Duncan's son gets the blame, he becomes king and all will soon be forgotten. "Or are you a coward?" his wife throws at him.

Macbeth carries out his plan and does indeed become king. But, of course, all is not forgotten. The heirs of Banquo, his closest brother in arms, would after all, according to the witches' prophesy, also become king. That must be avoided. An assassin will soon solve that, and Macbeth will be able to reign in peace. But the attempt on Banquo and his kin is only partially successful, and Banquo's son Fleance manages to escape. After this, Macbeth and his wife slowly become consumed by guilt and paranoia. This leads to their ultimate demise, but not before they have sent half of Scotland into the abyss, leaving a trail of death and destruction behind them.

Power corrupts; absolute power corrupts absolutely. This is one of the main themes of literature. Think, for example, of *Animal Farm* and Wagner's *Ring* cycle - he who wears the ring of power cannot help but be changed by it. That applies to almost anyone. A perfect example of the influence of power on ordinary people is the infamous Stanford Prison Experiment carried out by Professor Zimbardo in 1971. Twelve subjects were assigned at random the role of prisoner; twelve others were assigned the role of prison guard. After only a few days, the prison guards, who had been allowed to wear the ring of power, began to seriously misbehave towards the 'prisoners', so much so, in fact, that the experiment had to be prematurely ended. Under the wrong circumstances, therefore, most of us have it in us to be corrupted by power.

These same processes are reflected in industry. Macbeth would make a great management trainee and, with his decisiveness and successes, would make rapid headway in modern organizations. Planting a knife in the boss's back in a bid to gain absolute power no longer happens today, at least not literally. But leaking the right information to the right people works too – simpler, and at least as effective. In books such as *Barbarians at the Gate*,[19] Shakespeare's classic royal drama is given a new lick of paint. Even modern-day Macbeths will meet their end, but they too will usually leave a trail of destruction behind them: megalomaniac building projects, paralyzing business mergers, poisoned organizations.

Jansons steers clear of absolute power. He makes a conscious decision not to stand in front of the orchestra too often: "I want to keep them hungry. For me, it's important that I don't force myself on people, but that they actually want to work with me. My biggest fear, after nine years as chief conductor, is that a certain routine starts to creep into our relationship, and that the orchestra's hunger disappears. I try to avoid that in every way I can."

But even as chief conductor of the RCO – or whoever else in the organization might want to wield absolute power – it simply would not be possible. Power is distributed among a number of people, boards and committees, which hold each other in check. In this way, the RCO makes sure that a potential Macbeth could never hold the orchestra in his thrall. In Chapter Five, we will delve deeper into the structures that the RCO and other iconic organizations have set up to create and maintain distributed leadership and so to guarantee that their leaders are complementary and not authoritarian. But first, in Chapter Four, we will discuss how a team of the right people, led in the right way so that everyone feels responsible, can become iconic by delivering unparalleled results and sustaining them over time.

---

[19] Bryan Burrough and John Helyar (1989) *Barbarians at the Gate: The Fall of RJR Nabisco.* Harper & Row.

CHAPTER 4

# TIME

STEINWAY & SONS

Henri Steinway in 1967, the last CEO from the family

This chapter is about achieving unparalleled results for longer than deemed possible. The main driver and vital building block of the Circle of Iconic Competence is an unwavering aspiration to redefine the possible. Hubris and complacency are the human traits that stand in the way at this stage: someone who is successful can easily imagine that they are infallible and take their success for granted. Any organization that wants to remain iconic must prevent this from happening.

# On World Tour

It's 2009 and Jan Raes, who became managing director of the Concertgebouw Orchestra the year before, has organized an away-day for himself and
the rest of the management team so they can get started on an action plan for
2010-2014. The team is making a list of priorities based on an assessment of
current strengths and weaknesses of the orchestra by the foundation board,
the association board, the artistic committee and others involved in the orchestra. The four priorities are – in order of importance – conducting policy,
innovation, education, and income generation. For each priority, specific
actions are being proposed for implementation in the years to follow.

It is a completely open brainstorm – people can shout out anything they
like. In the course of the day, someone in the group – nobody can remember exactly who – came up with the idea of going on a world tour. The
RCO would become the first symphony orchestra to visit all six continents
in a single year, and when better to do this than in 2013, the orchestra's
125th anniversary year? It would also fit perfectly with the orchestra's priorities. Fueled by wine and ambition, the rest of the evening is given over
to imagining how the idea would work.

In the days that follow, Raes mulls the idea over in his mind. Of course, it
would be fantastic to do it – especially since Asia and South America are the
world's biggest growth markets for classical music; the orchestra has been
going on tour since 1895 and with a world tour, the orchestra would be able
to fulfill a number of long-cherished wishes to play to enthusiastic audiences
in emerging economies. But would they be successful this time in organizing
appearances in Australia, where before they had failed? Or in Africa, where
the orchestra had never played before? And how would the foundation
board react to the idea of organizing such a financially-risky venture in times
of crisis and cost cutting? And what about the members of the orchestra?
The number of travel days would exceed what was agreed in the orchestra
regulations; would they be prepared to make an exception in this case?

Raes begins by testing the waters with the chairs of the foundation board
and the orchestra members' association. To his relief, they respond enthusiastically to the idea. Next, he approaches Jansons, the chief-conductor. He is
immediately taken by the idea and is keen to lead the orchestra on a number
of the visits; for him, it is the realization of a childhood dream. Raes proceeds

to make a plan, put together a budget and talk to people. The Dutch Ministry of Foreign Affairs is enthusiastic and ready to help. Australia seems on the cards and Africa too! Slowly but surely the idea evolves from pipe dream to plan. Everyone gets that Richard Branson feeling: *screw it, let's do it!* The foundation board is willing to take the risk and gives the green light.

Four years later, the orchestra is playing one of its first concerts of the tour in that other temple of classical music, the Wiener Musikverein, home to the Vienna Philharmonic Orchestra. "You don't hear much Mahler here," remarks an old Viennese lady. "For me, that was reason enough to come. The orchestra and Mariss Jansons were another two. Not that there's anything wrong with our own Vienna Philharmonic, but their beauty is mainly in the violins, in my opinion. Here the energy comes from the whole orchestra. For me, the Concertgebouw Orchestra is a *Gesamtkunstwerk*."[1]

## One of a Kind

If you want to become iconic, then simply having a team of the right people who work well together is not enough, it is merely a necessary condition on the ascent to the top. In this chapter, we will deal with how to become iconic and how to stay that way, through a process of continuous improvement and balancing tradition and innovation. This is at the same time the beginning and the end of the circle of iconic competence: continually working to achieve unparalleled results is the goal of any iconic organization, but is in itself also a necessary condition to attract the right people and, in that way, to get the virtuous circle turning hence sustain iconic status.

To achieve unparalleled results, you have to start delivering work that is qualitatively of the highest level. In a leading orchestra, the measures of quality include evenness of rhythm, finding the right musical colours, crystal clear intonation, continuously striking the right balance between melody

---

[1]  M. Spel (2013). 'Dit orkest is een Gesamtkunstwerk'. *NRC Handelsblad*, 1 February.

and accompaniment and an unequalled flexibility and ability to adapt. This flexibility is so extreme that, in the spring of 2012 at the Barbican in London, the orchestra decided at the last moment to play a piece without a conductor. Jansons had fallen ill just before the interval, in a concert that had Richard Strauss' *Metamorphosen* on the programme – a composition for no fewer than 23 solo string players – each with their own separate part. The audience probably thought the orchestra had always intended to play the piece without a conductor, and afterwards Jansons luckily felt well enough to go on and conduct *the Rosenkavalier*.

Achieving the highest quality demands a huge amount of practice and preparation. "I always prepare, very thoroughly," says Jansons. "I really have to get into a piece, get inside it."[2] Jansons has been preparing since he was a small child. From a young age, he attended the rehearsals of his father, Arvid Jansons, conductor at the Riga opera, the Latvian Radio Orchestra and later at the Leningrad Philharmonic. As a child, he played a game where he would take a real musical score and direct his own little 'orchestra' of buttons. "I put together whole programmes and rehearsed them, after which I would direct the orchestra to leave the stage and return a few moments later for the concert."[3] Over the past 60 years, Jansons has clearly put in a multiple of the 10,000 hours of training that Malcolm Gladwell determined as necessary to reach the top in any discipline.[4]

But unparalleled results are about more than just top quality. They need that 'special something' that makes those results unusual and unique in the world. For the Concertgebouw Orchestra, it is the ability to perform a broad repertoire at a very high level, and to inspire audiences with it. "The Concertgebouw Orchestra has a chameleon-like quality," writes music editor Thiemo Wind. "It can adapt itself to a conductor like no other, and it can sound the way he or she wishes. What's more, the orchestra has the courage to show its soft underbelly, which allows it to add a unique sensitivity and depth to its game." Conductor Valery Gergiev finds that the orchestra moulds itself so closely to the beat of his baton that he compares conducting it to playing the piano.

---

[2]  Kettle (2004).

[3]  Kettle (2004).

[4]  M. Gladwell (2008). *Outliers: The Story of Success.* London: Penguin Books.

Finally, unparalleled results are never static – what is unparalleled today will no longer be so tomorrow. The RCO is careful never to fall into routine. It doesn't want to become a museum piece, but remains an orchestra that continually improves and adapts itself. This continuous drive to ever-greater levels of quality contains perhaps the deepest essence of iconicity.

Just as in the previous two chapters, we shall begin by discussing an example (Steinway, the legendary piano maker) to introduce the themes in this chapter. Next, we will discuss the three building blocks that describe how organizations can achieve continuously evolving, unparalleled results.

Sudden Mania to become Pianists created upon hearing STEINWAY's Pianos at the Paris Exposition.

**Figure 4-1**    Engraving. Chaotic scenes as crowds fight to get near the new Steinway piano at the 1867 World Exhibition in Paris.

# Steinway: Builder of the World's Most Iconic Concert Pianos

In 1853, Heinrich Engelhard Steinweg (later anglicized to Steinway) started his company with the stated ambition of building the best pianos in the world at an acceptable cost price.[5] Within the space of two decades, this combination of perfectionism and pragmatism made the company a leading piano manufacturer. The Paris World Exhibition of 1867 even suffered a stampede when Steinway presented his newest grand piano. "A son of Mr. Steinway stood by the instruments at the Exhibition and ensured that they kept being played at all times," reads the jury report. "The exhibition-goers were so charmed by its sound that for months they were present without a pause and in great numbers." The jury was no less intrigued by the power and charm of these instruments. Even *La Gazette Musicale de Paris* wrote about the fascination. As a consequence, the only prize to be awarded during this exhibition went to Mr Steinway.[6]

The stampede in Paris came about because Steinway had introduced radical improvements to the piano's design – at that time, the piano was the instrument chosen *par excellence* to bring music into the living rooms of the growing middle classes. It was the nineteenth-century equivalent of a stereo system. But whereas a soft, round tone sufficed for the drawing room, it was not enough for the concert halls, which were growing ever larger. The grand pianos of the time simply could not provide the power and volume that was required. For example, the great piano virtuoso Franz Liszt demanded two grand pianos per concert, so that he could quickly move to a second instrument if too many strings and hammers broke on the first.[7] Steinway was the first piano producer to solve these problems and design a piano that combined a beautiful sound with good volume and reliable body strength.

Steinway senior worked together with his sons to introduce a number of essential innovations and in doing so re-invented the piano as the instrument we know today. "Heinrich was a man who researched, experimented,

---

[5]   S. Kotha & R. Dunbar (1997). *Steinway & Sons*. Stern School of Business, NY University.

[6]   M. Chevalier (1868). *Rapports du Jury International, Exposition Universelle de 1867 à Paris*, red. Tome deuxième, Groupe II, Classes 6 à 13, p. 231.

[7]   D. Gooley (2004). *The Virtuoso Listz*. Cambridge University Press, p. 108.

and then moved at speed," says Werner Husmann, who today heads Steinway in Europe and Asia. "And he passed this mentality on to his sons." Heinrich was the first to place the strings diagonally in a grand piano. In this way, the bass strings came to be positioned closer to the middle of the soundboard, so that their vibration was amplified. But it was Steinway's son Theodore who perfected this vibration when he developed a production method that made it possible to produce the inner and outer rims of the piano in a single step. In this way, a wooden structure was developed which responds as a single body and optimally strengthens the vibration of the strings, just like a violin.

Producing the inner and outer rim of a Steinway grand piano in a single step, in the way that Theodore Steinway had patented in 1880 and which is unique to Steinway even today.

Because Steinway's production method was very expensive, the company needed to create economies of scale to keep the price acceptable. For instance, it was only possible to work with perfect pieces of wood seven metres long with the grain in the length. Also, from the beginning of the production process, a complete piano case had to be transported through the factory at each successive step. The investments that were needed were substantial.

William Steinway, another of Heinrich's sons, played an important role in capturing the top slice of the market. He built a concert hall in Manhattan with no less than 2,500 seats, at a time when renowned piano builders such as Pleyel and Erard in Paris had concert halls that could seat no more than 200 listeners.[8] Thanks to the size of the Steinway Hall, the company succeeded not only in attracting the best pianists who gave crucial feedback, but also in adjusting the instruments perfectly to the demands of a large hall.

As soon as the company achieved market leadership in the top segment of grand pianos, it gained a long-lasting competitive advantage: any competitor would have great difficulty in generating the scale that was needed to earn back the huge costs in a market where Steinway was lord and master.

The quality DNA that Steinway senior had injected into his company was first put to the test in 1880 when growth in the number of musicians in the middle classes led to an explosion in demand for upright pianos in people's living rooms. Theodore wanted to enter this fast-growing market for cheaper pianos; his brother William, however, succeeded in maintaining Steinway's course as a pure producer of top-quality pianos.[9] Two decades later, this scenario repeated itself when Steinway decided to steer clear of the promising market for self-playing pianolas.

Looking back, these decisions to remain focused on the top segment of the market were the right ones. The arrival of radio from 1920 caused the market for pianolas to dry up, and the crisis of 1929 did the same for upright pianos. The majority of the 1,400 piano makers that were around at the turn of the twentieth century went bust.[10]

In 1972, after 120 years as a family business, Steinway's quality DNA was again put to the test when the company was sold to CBS, a large American media group. The piano market was under pressure from a number of sources, including the rise of low-cost Japanese producers and product substitution by electric pianos. The many descendants of the Steinway family who owned the shares were unwilling or unable to make the necessary investments in the company. The takeover by the well-capitalized CBS seemed like a neat solution. Following the takeover, long-overdue investments in production capacity were indeed made.

CBS took a number of measures to earn back its investment, including cutting costs. This was hardly surprising, as the process used to build a Steinway is notoriously labour and capital intensive. For example, Steinway employs its own wood specialists who buy the best quality wood on the world markets. Following purchase, the wood must dry out for between 12 and 24 months, and half of it is rejected even then because the quality is not good enough. It was these sorts of enormous costs and demands on capital that CBS hoped to reduce. Furthermore, CBS tried to increase revenues, for example by quickly expanding the distribution network. In doing so, it relaxed the demands that Steinway had traditionally placed on the expertise of the piano dealers.[11]

CBS policy proved disastrous. Sales and profit did at first rise, but Steinway's reputation suffered. Pianists began to cast doubt onto Steinway's quality, and a lively trade grew up in 50-year old Steinway grand pianos.[12] Between 1977 and 1985, CBS hired four different new managing directors to set the company straight – as many new leaders as had led the company in the preceding 120 years – but with every new managing director, the trust that customers and employees had placed in the firm diminished still further.[13] Morale in the company sank to an all-time low when

[8]  A. Walker, *Franz Liszt: The Virtuoso Years, 1811-1847*, Cornell University Press, 1983.

[9]  Steinway did indeed start producing upright pianos, but only of the very best quality, and therefore not aimed at the mass market. Moreover, these pianos only ever represented a small part of Steinway's turnover.

[10]  Alfred Dolge (1911). *Pianos and their Makers*. Covina Publishing Company.

[11]  J.T. Gourville & J.B. Lassiter III (2000). *Steinway & Sons: Buying a Legend*. Harvard Business School.

[12]  Kotha & Dunbar (1997).

[13]  Gourville & Lassiter (2000).

CBS closed its music division, and finally sold Steinway, after a long and poorly-conducted sales process.[14]

Despite the bruised confidence of the public and the firm's employees, the quality of Steinway's DNA appeared so intact that the company was able to regain its old stature: the employees' high regard for traditional quality formed the basis for a healthy discussion with the new management: production methods were only modernized if it helped improve quality. Even the company's harshest critics at the *New York Times* wrote in 1995: "A recent tour of the Steinway factory in Queens showed an apparently serious effort to improve the instrument. The final stages of manufacture receive more attention than they did a few years ago. Outside technicians have also reported improvements in Steinways, a heartening sign."[15]

Steinway did not only overhaul its production process, but also its distribution network. Only the very best distributors retained permission to sell Steinways. In the United States the number of distributors was reduced from 153 to 110. They were required to show the old senses of professionalism, stature and quality that were in keeping with Steinway. The dealers' piano technicians, for example, were required first to complete a five-day training session in the factories in New York or Hamburg. In this way, Steinway actively extended its circle of competence to include its distributors.

On 19 September 2013, Steinway (having been publicly owned since 1996) was taken over by John Paulson. Although he was an expert in taking over and drastically restructuring companies in need, his motivation in taking over Steinway was of quite a different kind. "If you have something that is perfect and that occupies an unparalleled position in the sector, then you don't want to mess it up. Both my sisters were good pianists and they dreamed of a Steinway. My father couldn't afford it and bought them a small grand piano – not a Steinway. I recall my sisters crying when the piano was being delivered. I realized then for the first time what kind of

---

[14] CBS allowed the sales process to drag on almost interminably, and it was even rumoured that CBS intended to dispose of the Steinway factories for their real estate value. E. Rothstein (1988). *To Make a Piano It Takes More Than Tools*. Smithsonian.

[15] E. Rothstein (1995). 'Made in the USA, Once Gloriously, Now Precariously'. *The New York Times*, 28 May.

[16] Kotha & Dunbar (1997).

attraction Steinway exerts on musicians. My aim is to protect Steinway and safeguard the instruments' quality."

Steinway is once again the icon that it has been for the majority of its 160-year history. The vast majority of piano concerts in famous concert halls are still performed on Steinways.[16]

# The Three Building Blocks of Unparalleled Results Over Time

As with the other steps in the circle of iconic competence, we shall now synthesize the elements that we see consistently reflected in the iconic organizations we have studied. The three elements shown below form the requirements that organizations need to become and remain iconic (see *Figure 4-2*).

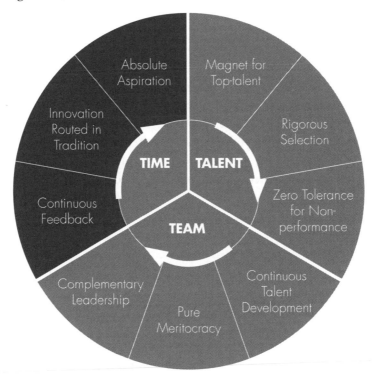

**Figure 4-2**   The three elements in the Circle of Iconic Competence that give rise to unparalleled results consistently over time.

## 1. Continuous Feedback

Continuous development, which we discussed in the previous chapter, can only take place through continuous feedback, both on an individual and a team level. Head chef Adrià of elBulli restaurant constantly tastes his chefs' ingredients, half-finished products and dishes, and he also listens to how guests respond to the dishes. McKinsey evaluates and trains its consultants constantly (as is necessary for its up-or-out policy) and gathers continuous feedback from its clients who may or may not buy new projects, depending on their level of satisfaction. The All Blacks players can watch video pictures of a match on their own computers to see what went well and what they can improve upon. And at Steinway the piano makers receive immediate feedback on the quality of their concert pianos from the world's best pianists who play them.

In the RCO, exchanging feedback between the musicians is an almost automatic process. "Evaluation is constant, because in an orchestra, you are always sticking your neck out," says oboist Kouwenhoven. "Everyone can see how well you did during a rehearsal or a concert, and you immediately know yourself how well you have done." Furthermore, everyone can review their own performance on CD, radio and television and also receive feedback from the press, the audience and friends of the orchestra.

The musicians also give each other regular feedback on their playing, says bass player Seldis: "For example, I wouldn't hesitate to speak to a trombonist if I thought he could up his game. In other orchestras, they wouldn't dream of it ('You're a strings player. What do you know about it?'). These suggestions are simply regarded as ways to get better together; there's no question of a right-or-wrong mentality." The musicians are in fact quite reticent about giving feedback to each other. The most important thing is that they feel free to play, so they are keen to avoid the rise of a blame culture, which would stand in their way. Most feedback actually takes place implicitly and nonverbally, by "osmosis", as former chairman of the board Reibestein so elegantly puts it.

On a team level the rehearsals are an important form of feedback for orchestras. "Rehearsals are like meditative moments," says Dieter Flury of the Vienna Philharmonic. "At rehearsals we practise together, but you don't yet feel the pressure to play to the best of your ability – and so you have more room to take risks." In this sense, orchestral rehearsals are comparable to training sessions in a sports team, or the testing of recipes in a restaurant.

Guest conductors also play an important role in the feedback process, which in their case is a two-way street. On the one hand, they play an important role in the learning process of the orchestra as a whole. "Outstanding guest conductors, such as Nikolaus Harnoncourt and Kirill Kondrashin, have contributed to the development of the RCO sound culture," says editor Bert Koopman. On the other hand, guest conductors are also evaluated by the orchestra; after a guest conductorship, the orchestra members give their feedback, which is then discussed in the artistic committee. In this way, the RCO works constantly to attract the best guest conductors to work with the orchestra, so that they continue to learn as much as they can as a team.

Finally, audience reactions to concerts are, without doubt, a very important feedback mechanism for group performance. Audience reactions are, of course, immediately noticeable – lots of coughing during a concert or lukewarm applause at the end are not good signs – and the reviews the following day are also studied very closely. "Everyone reads what's written in the following day's newspaper," says Reibestein. "If reviewers in important newspapers write for example 'the brass section was disappointing last night' or 'the RCO has been doing more or less the same thing for a long time now', that is important input for both the musicians and for the leaders who determine policy." The same thing applies at the Vienna Philharmonic. "We pay attention not so much to odd pieces of positive or negative feedback, but more to the tendency in the comments," says Flury. He also points out that the number of invitations from concert organizers – or the lack of them – is also an important indicator for the orchestra.

Feedback on group performance is, of course, also essential for success in industry. Almost all companies pay close attention to their quarterly results. The best companies, however, also look at other figures when measuring the success of the company as a whole – this is because it can take years before problems in, say, customer satisfaction or product development express themselves in poorer financial results. By that time it is often too late. Scania, the Swedish truck manufacturer, keeps in direct touch with truck drivers to get constant feedback over its products – and to be able to respond immediately when there is a problem. Furthermore,

Scania has an extensive system in place to monitor and improve efficiency in its factories. This system also helps to compare business operations in different factories with one another and to act on lessons learned.[17] These feedback mechanisms play an important role in Scania's success.

## 2. Innovation Rooted in Tradition

Finding the right balance between continuing to do what you're good at and going in search of something new is perhaps the most important strategic challenge for organizations. Research into the decline of 40 initially successful organizations showed that in more than 90% of cases, the decline was due to their striking the wrong balance between focus and innovation.[18] Almost two-thirds of the companies involved in this research met their demise as a result of unbridled growth, even though their core activities were healthy – well-known examples are the French water company Vivendi, which nearly went bust because it wanted to reinvent itself as a media conglomerate, and America's biggest insurance company, AIG, which had to be rescued by the government because it had bitten off more than it could chew in its desire to grow from a seller of traditional insurance policies into a provider of complex financial products such as derivatives. At the other end of the spectrum, almost 30% of companies were too slow to innovate, often just as their core activities came under severe pressure. Kodak, for example, did not succeed in carving out a strong position for itself in the digital world (something which rival Fuji did manage to do)[19] and had to file for bankrupcy.

In iconic organizations, tradition is important for continuity and success. But 'tradition' must never be used as an excuse to stand in the way of necessary innovation. Chief conductor of the Berlin Philharmonic, Simon Rattle, puts it like this: "The whole point of tradition is to take what is strongest and most vital and transport it to a new world. We are all searching for what that is." This observation is also very apt for a company like Steinway, which is making improvements to a traditional production method that is over a hundred years old by selectively making use of the most advanced computer-controlled apparatus which, in certain essential steps in the production process, achieves a level of precision that is simply not attainable by hand and which further improves the quality of the classic Steinway grand piano.

The importance of tradition and the level of focus that goes with it are unmistakable. "You always have to place the strategy within the history of the company," says Unilever CEO Paul Polman. "Don't talk about changing everything. People join and stay with companies because they are very proud of that company's history, traditions and its ways of working ... I always talked about the change as rediscovering the greatness of our history."[20] Following his appointment, Polman traveled the world communicating a number of simple, shared goals to the company he now led. Unilever's *Sustainable Living Plan* encapsulates the way in which Unilever aimed to continue producing unparalleled results. On the one hand, the goal was to do this by being a growth entity that provides and creates jobs and that helps improve welfare in the countries in which it operates. And on the other, the company sought to use that same growth as a means to shape active sustainability in different dimensions; not only by reducing its environmental impact, but also – and most importantly – by increasing people's sense of wellbeing. In 2008, just as the financial crisis was unfolding, Unilever decided to exchange the pressure of reporting quarterly results – *three-month rat races* in the words of Polman – for a long-term business plan based on sustainability.[21] In the four years that followed, the share price of the company doubled.

Jansons, too, sees how the long history of the Concertgebouw Orchestra extends its workings into the modern world: "I think you can still hear something of the Mengelberg sound even today. His gentle and noble way of making music, which I recognize from old recordings ... I can still hear it even today. You can also hear something of Haitink and Chailly in the sound. Journalists have often asked me: 'What are you going to change?' But I prefer instead to work with what is already there, and make it

---

[17] Zook (2012).

[18] Zook (2012).

[19] K.N.C. (2012). *Sharper focus: how Fujifilm survived. The Economist*, 18 January.

[20] Summarized from Zook (2012), p. 173.

[21] Unilever (2013). *Unilever 2013 in de Benelux: Samen duurzaam groeien*, http://www.unilever.nl/Images/Unilever-in-de-Benelux-2013_tcm164-343139.pdf, accessed on 17 March 2013. D. Zabarenko (2013). 'CEO Paul Polman from Unilever on ending the "three month rat-race"'. *Thomson Reuters*, blog, http://blog.thomsonreuters.com/index.php/executive-perspective-ceo-paul-polman-from-unilever-on-ending-the-three-month-rat-race, accessed on 17 March 2013.

better. And of course change does come out of that." It is interesting that the orchestra still retains something of the Mengelberg sound, because of course nobody from that era (more than 65 years ago) still plays in the orchestra today. The feat recalls the ship of Theseus in classical Athens. This renowned ship was preserved and maintained as a relic, with every rotting plank replaced. After many years, there was not a single plank left from the original ship, and yet it still remained in some way the ship of Theseus.

Passing on the old sound tradition, which is also closely related to the world-renowned acoustics of the Concertgebouw concert hall, is essential to the RCO. "But," adds Jansons, "it must never become routine. I never want to perform the same piece of music more than three or four times in a row. On concert tours you sometimes have to do more. I find that hard. In those cases, I try each night to change or improve something." The Concertgebouw Orchestra wants to keep the old sound and at the same time to renew it.

The following anecdote, told by cellist Julia Tom, summarizes this ambivalence beautifully: "We still play from the old Mahler scores from the time of Mengelberg. His notes are still in there, written in blue pencil. That is of course amazing – no other orchestra has anything like that – but also a bit awkward. You can't erase the blue pencil if you want to change something."

Fortunately, not everything in the orchestra is as difficult to erase as blue pencil, and much has changed since Mengelberg. In fact, the orchestra used to be known as a "conductor eater", whereas it is now better known for its chameleon-like ability to work with very different types of conductors. Furthermore, the repertoire has been considerably extended, both out of a love for modern music (a love that in the 1960s was pretty much on the rocks) and in the introduction of authentic performance methods for baroque and classical music, such as that composed by Johann Sebastian Bach or Wolfgang Amadeus Mozart. Nikolaus Harnoncourt in particular has played an important role in this for the orchestra since 1975.

In recent years too the orchestra has worked very hard to move with the times. It has worked more with younger conductors, it has more 20- and 30-year-olds among its members and it has become much more international: over 20 different nationalities are now represented in the orchestra.

The orchestra has also set up its own music label, *RCO Live*, and holds many innovative concerts, such as in the interdisciplinary AAA Series, the introductory concerts for new audiences, and the King's Night Concert,[22] performed together with musicians from different genres.

One of the biggest challenges faced by the RCO is the decline in popularity of classical music among young people. In an attempt to reach out to this group, the orchestra has set up an extensive educational programme, launched new initiatives and promoted a young people's group called Entrée. It also went on its world tour in its anniversary year, an opportunity to reach new audiences worldwide and share a love of music with them.

But alongside these innovations, the orchestra still plays Mahler and Beethoven; the renowned B Series continues to form the bedrock of its programme, and it will continue to refine and improve its classical repertoire. In its own words, the orchestra is both "museum and laboratory".[23]

There is no simple answer to the question of what the right balance is between tradition and innovation – it depends on market conditions (is there much or little change?) and the situation the organization is in (is it healthy or in imminent danger?). In the Concertgebouw Orchestra you do hear a continuous discussion between different people and committees about where the orchestra should innovate and where it should hold onto tradition. Some want more Dutch composers, others want more modern music, and yet others feel the orchestra should keep more classical music in its repertoire, because that is where the most refined sound culture is to be found, and because it is the easiest way to draw big enough audiences. There is no right answer – what matters is that the discussion goes on. An iconic organization only really comes into danger if the discussion about the balance between tradition and renewal ceases, and one of the two is neglected.

---

[22] A concert held on the eve of King's Day, a Dutch public holiday to celebrate the anniversary of the King's inauguration.

[23] M. Cleij & M. van Dongen (2013). 'Componisten over de vloer' (p. 158-175). In: Khalifa (2013).

## 3. Absolute Aspiration

One might almost expect the musicians in the RCO to aspire to be better than the Vienna Philharmonic or the Berlin Philharmonic. Nothing could be further from the truth; the musicians show surprisingly little interest in the competition. The Concertgebouw Orchestra wants first and foremost to better *itself*: the musicians are keen to do better than their last concert, time and time again. "We always measure ourselves against our own best performance, and not that of others," says lead bassist Dominic Seldis. "That also helps make sure we don't fall into complacency – we should always improve upon our own benchmark. We keep on polishing the diamond."

*This absolute aspiration* is an essential ingredient for iconic organizations, an ingredient that we had not originally expected. Most companies, after all, seem to focus on beating the competition. Keeping an eye on your competitors is of course also important for success. But those who measure themselves against other organizations can logically speaking never be innovative, and also never iconic. Added to this is that those who have only a relative aspiration ("to beat the competition") can sit back on their laurels once they have done that. An organization with absolute aspiration ("to be better than itself") never eases up on its drive to improve, a drive that is necessary to remain iconic.

The RCO's ambition is absolute, and achieving the status of best orchestra in the world in no way detracts from the orchestra's will to become even better. "In the beginning, Jansons had mixed feelings about achieving first place in the *Gramophone* ratings," says percussionist Rieken. "Of course, he was pleased with the recognition. But he was also afraid the orchestra would fall into complacency. Though I haven't seen anything of the sort. Everyone remains passionate and emotional about the orchestra and the quest for magical concerts."

We see the same absolute ambition in iconic organizations in industry. IKEA founder Ingvar Kamprad, for instance, constantly urged his employees on: *Most things remain to be done. A glorious future!* And of course Steinway, which with its innovations has redefined not only the grand piano itself, but also the piano industry. The company saw itself as elevated so far above the competition that in 1893 it refused to stand among the 'ordinary' piano builders at the Chicago World Exhibition (in the same way that Steven Jobs refused to stand at CeBIT, the biggest exhibition for consumer electronics). However, the Polish piano legend Ignacy Jan Pederewski, who topped the bill at the opening ceremony, would only play on a Steinway – very much to the dismay of the exhibition organizers. In that way, Steinway at least 'won' a PR victory, by not taking part in the competition.[24]

Absolute aspiration is an extension of an organization's competence. Bringing better classical music to the stage, or better rugby to the pitch, are excellent ambitions to have. But the ambition to be the most profitable orchestra or rugby team would almost certainly have a detrimental effect, because this kind of performance is merely *consequential*. That is also one of the biggest differences between organizations such as the RCO and the All Blacks on the one hand, and regular companies on the other. Financial health and competition do of course play a very prominent role in companies, and this makes it more difficult to strive to achieve pure ambition when it comes to meeting client needs. This challenge arises especially when a company suffers a setback and the financial situation requires urgent attention – this is precisely the moment at which the temptation to abandon absolute aspiration is greatest, and at the same time is potentially most damaging.

# When Money Takes Centre Stage

Money plays an important role, even in the lives of iconic organizations. The Concertgebouw Orchestra, elBulli and other organizations cannot afford to ignore their financial situation; if they did, they would soon go under. That applies of course even more strongly to companies who need profit to invest and to keep their shareholders happy.

But money must never be allowed to take centre stage. "There is always an intrinsic tension between business and art," says former RCO director Jan Willem Loot. "The trick is to put artistic interest first and to fit that into the business interest."

---

[24] S. Kotha & R. Dunbar (1997).

We see comparable principles in other iconic organizations. "Profit gives us resources," IKEA founder Kamprad tells his organization. Profit is therefore absolutely not a dirty word; on the contrary, profit is necessary for continued existence and growth. But it remains a means to an end, and not an end in itself. The goal is to develop affordable furniture for all, and profit is a necessary means to achieve it. At Steinway we saw the same: the highest-quality grand pianos for a reasonable profit.

It is a constant paradox that some of the most profitable companies are those least focused on making a profit. Apple, the darling of the stock exchange between 2000 and 2010, was not in the least bit interested in shareholder value – Steve Jobs' contempt for analysts and investors was legendary.

Hubris, greed and selfish ambition are, however, deeply rooted in the human psyche, and those who are doing well can easily delude themselves that they are immune to disaster. Toyota is a prime example. The Japanese car manufacturer is the inventor of *lean manufacturing*, embodied in its Toyota Production System. Since the 1950s, the company has strived to make ever better cars at ever-lower cost. In the 1980s and 1990s, this brought Toyota so much success that global market leadership was in sight. The company decided that this must become its new goal, and made every effort to become the biggest. What happened next is well known: the company reached its goal – fleetingly – and at enormous cost: the once legendary quality of the cars could no longer be taken for granted, and Toyota was forced into large-scale product recalls.

In February 2010, Toyota was called to account in the American Congress, where the firm's newly-appointed president, Akio Toyoda, testified as follows:[25] "I would like to discuss what caused the recall issues we are facing now. Toyota has, for the past few years, been expanding its business rapidly. Quite frankly, I fear the pace at which we have grown may have been too quick. I would like to point out here that Toyota's priority has traditionally been the following: First: Safety, Second: Quality, and Third: Volume. These priorities became confused, and we were not able to stop, think, and make improvements as much as we were able to before, and our basic stance to listen to customers' voices to make better products has weakened somewhat. We pursued growth over the speed at which we were able to develop our people and our organization, and we should sincerely be mindful of that ... Since last June, when I first took office, I have personally placed the highest priority on improving quality over quantity, and I have shared that direction with our stakeholders. As you well know, I am the grandson of the founder, and all the Toyota vehicles bear my name. For me, when the cars are damaged, it is as though I am as well. I, more than anyone, wish for Toyota's cars to be safe, and for our customers to feel safe when they use our vehicles."

There are few leaders who dare to be so honest about the mistakes their company has made, and who want to work openly to revive their quality DNA. We hope that this book will encourage executives to look into the mirror and ask themselves: Are we remaining true to the core values our organization stands for? Or has the achievement of short-term financial goals perhaps become too important? Is there enough room for discussion in our organization to strike the right balance between focus and innovation? Is there any chance we have become overconfident?

[25] *The Guardian* (2010). 'Toyota president Akio Toyoda's statement to Congress'. guardian.co.uk, 24 February, http://www.guardian.co.uk/business/2010/feb/24/akio-toyoda-statement-to-congress, accessed on 8 February 2013. This text includes two extracts from the speech.

# CHAPTER 5

# ORGANIZING THE CIRCLE OF ICONIC COMPETENCE

Wilbert and Vieve Gore, founders of W.L. Gore & Associates, inventors of Gore-Tex

This chapter is about similarities between iconic organizations in the way they uphold the Circle of Iconic Competence. In particular, the German idea of *Mitbestimmung* (often translated as 'co-determination' or 'participative management') seems to be at the heart of the long-term maintenance of iconic status. This concept anchors the circle firmly in the whole organization, making it much less dependent on a few individuals.

In the previous three chapters, we dealt with the three sections Talent, Team and Time of the circle of iconic competence, and the total of nine elements that make them up. In this chapter, we will look at how icons organize themselves to keep the virtuous circle going. The parts we will discuss form important conditions for keeping the circle turning and making it run faster, so that unparalleled results can lead to iconic status. As with the main elements in the circle, we have distilled these conditions from the organizations we have studied. Moreover, we have found that they are surprisingly universal among the icons in business, culture, and sport.

Three components will be covered. First, the governance structure, which is important for making sure that a sense of responsibility for unparalleled results is distributed broadly across the organization, so that power can never fall into a single person's hands. Then comes the importance of social cohesion in iconic organizations and ways to foster it. Third comes the *common thread* that runs through the circle of competence, the organization and circumstances: in iconic organizations, all the pieces of the jigsaw fit together and are mutually reinforcing.

In Chapter Three we discussed the importance of complementary leadership. The conductor, the orchestra and all the environmental factors reinforce each other to produce unparalleled results. To sustain this, you need a governance structure that prevents one-sided interests from gaining the upper hand over time. This is why many iconic organizations have a form of distributed leadership. We will start off by looking at the example of W.L. Gore. This is a well known example of a large, leading organization with an iconic product where leadership is completely distributed, without the company lapsing into anarchy.

## The Innovative Democracy Behind Gore-Tex

Many people know Gore-Tex, but hardly anyone knows who makes it, the company W.L. Gore & Associates. And yet the company is every bit as remarkable as the waterproof but breathable fabric it produces. Gore has revenues over $3 billion and more than 10,000 employees. The company makes thousands of different products, including dental floss, components for fuel cells, glass fibre cables and many different sorts of special textile.[1]

It even makes medical products: more than 13 million heart patients carry Gore implants.[2] Most companies would set up a comprehensive governance structure to closely manage an enterprise with so many different products. But not Gore, where managers are hardly, if ever, appointed.

Wilbert (Bill) L. Gore founded the company together with his wife Genevieve (Vieve) in 1958, after he had left chemical giant DuPont, frustrated after 17 years of loyal service. He saw opportunities to use polytetrafluorethylene (PFTE) that his bosses did not see, and decided to take matters into his own hands. Not only did he hope to develop new applications for PFTE (better known as Teflon); he also dreamed of building a truly innovative organization, where people would not be held back by bureaucracy and rules. Instead of being led by appointed managers, his employees would be driven along by a combination of trust, peer pressure and an inner urge to invent good products.[3]

Gore, who died in 1986, appears to have been successful in his aim; more than 50 years after his company was founded, it is still free of bureaucracy and hierarchy. For instance, leaders are not appointed, but arise naturally if they are able to assemble enough followers behind them. CEO Terri Kelly is no exception: "We didn't even get a list of names – we were free to choose whomever we wanted within the company," she explains. "To my amazement, I was chosen."[4]

The system appears to work surprisingly well and represents an important factor in making the organization both innovative and selective at the same time. "If you can't persuade enough people to work on something, then maybe it's not such a great idea after all," says John Bacino, a membrane expert at Gore.[5] In this way, the company becomes a sort of innovation democracy, but one where the voters are experts and have a shared interest in the outcome.

---

[1]   http://www.gore.com, accessed on 7 December 2012.

[2]   Gary Hamel & Bill Breen (2007). *The Future of Management*. Boston, MA: Harvard Business School Publishing.

[3]   Simon Caulkin (2008). 'Gore-Tex gets made without managers'. *The Observer*, 2 November.

[4]   Caulkin (2008).

[5]   Ann Harrington (2003). 'Who's Afraid of a New Product?' *Fortune*, 10 November.

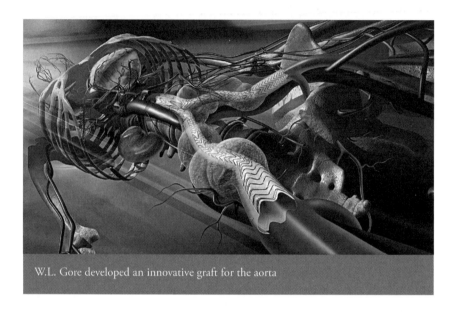

W.L. Gore developed an innovative graft for the aorta

Another special feature of the company is that hardly any of its locations employ more than 200 people. A department or factory that grows bigger than this number has to split off – in the words of Bill Gore: "You have to divide so you can multiply."[6] He believed that staying small is the only way to keep the feeling that '*we* have decided' instead of '*they* have decided'.[7] Everyone continues to feel responsible.

This sense of responsibility is also extended to financial management, in that all employees are joint owners. After a number of years all employees – who are known as *associates* – start to receive about 10% of their salary in the form of Gore shares. This has a clear effect on the attitude of the people within the company: "We always keep on talking about shareholder value when we are discussing plans," says employee John Kennedy.[8]

A final example of Gore's management philosophy is the 10% rule: every researcher is given that amount of work time to devote to developing new ideas. Most breakthroughs come from these projects. Gore's guitar strings are a good example: they are coated with PFTE (Teflon), so that less oil from the skin is deposited on the strings, which improves the sound quality. This new application was developed, in his 10% time, by an engineer who tested the concept by trying out the PFTE coating on the cables of his mountain bike.[9] Gore was one of the pioneers of the 10% rule: nowadays an increasing number of companies have a similar system. The best-known example is Google, where programmers can manage as much as 20% of their own time.

You might imagine that in such an unstructured organization, people with the loudest mouths are the one who are listened to most. "In practice, it just doesn't happen," says HR associate Anne Gillies. "There's a technical specialist in one plant who is very knowledgeable, and very uncommunicative. People accept it takes time to get his contribution because they know it's in their interest."[10]

Of course, not everyone finds their niche in this system. Many newcomers find themselves facing a difficult period at the end of the first year because, for example, they feel they are receiving too little guidance from the rest of the organization. But those who come through this often stay with Gore for many years. This is apparent from the many employer awards the company receives: it is a permanent fixture in the annual *Fortune* list of the hundred best companies to work for.

The nice thing about this employee satisfaction is that it does not come at a cost to the financial results: on the contrary. Gore has so far been profitable in every single year of its existence, and has tripled its revenues in the past 20 years: a steady growth rate of more than 5% per annum. Most publicly listed companies of similar size can only dream of such positive results over such a long period.

---

[6]   Harrington (2003).

[7]   Hamel & Breen (2007).

[8]   Formerly responsible for consumer textiles in Europe. *Cf.* Tom Lester (1993). 'The Gores Happy Family – WL Gore'. *Management Today*, 9 February.

[9]   Hamel & Breen (2007).

[10]   Lester (1993).

# Governance Structure

The distributed leadership we see at W.L. Gore can also be observed on a smaller scale in the Royal Concertgebouw Orchestra ( which has just under 200 people). Figure 5-1 shows a simplified version of the orchestra's governance structure. What is immediately striking is that the system is full of checks and balances: reporting lines run up, down and from side to side – no single entity has absolute power. What also stands out is that the system seems relatively complex for such a small organization. But – and so say all the musicians and staff members – the time that is needed for all the discussions more than pays for itself in the sense of responsibility that everyone feels for policy, and in the safety mechanisms the system produces. We will now discuss the different parts of this structure and how they work together to help keep the circle of iconic competence going.

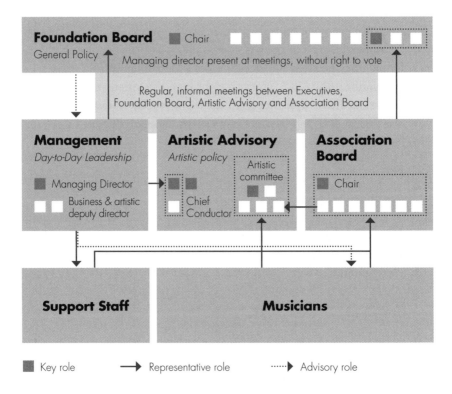

**Figure 5-1**   Checks and balances in the governance of the Concertgebouw Orchestra.

The *Management* leads the musicians and support staff of the orchestra on a day-to-day basis; its members are responsible for implementing policy, both artistic and commercial. In the past, the orchestra had two managing directors on the same level, one for artistic leadership and one for business. That did not work well in practice and regularly led to escalating conflict. "With Jan Willem Loot we merged the two functions into one managing director," says former member of the board Maarten van Veen. "The trade-offs between artistic and business interests have to be made by one and the same person." The managing director is appointed by and accountable to the Foundation Board.

The *Artistic Council* advises on artistic policy, on which pieces are played at concerts, with which conductors and soloists, and how the rehearsal schedule looks. The Council consists of the managing director, the deputy artistic advisor, the chief conductor and the Artistic Committee (AC), the latter comprising five members of the orchestra, one of whom is also on the Association Board. The managing director chairs the meetings, which take place roughly once every two months.

The *Association Board* is a special kind of entity. In formal terms, the board of the Concertgebouw Orchestra is a legally independent entity made up of members of the orchestra and staff. This association was set up in 1915 to represent the interests of the musicians and staff members to the management and chief conductor. The members choose the Association Board from their midst. The association is at the same time a *de facto* trade union, a works council and fellow member of the Management Board. It has played an important role over the course of the orchestra's history. In 1952, for example, it was closely involved in the organizational split between the orchestra and the concert hall.[11] "The Association Board is responsible for the good leadership of the orchestra," says chairman Herman Rieken. "It has a stabilising effect on the continuity of the orchestra, and ensures a common thread of history."

---

[11] E-mail from Bert Koopman, in the authors' possession.

The *Foundation Board* appoints the managing director, helps fill other key positions and determine policy, and controls and advises the management – it has a similar function to the supervisory board of a company. The Foundation Board interferes as little as possible with artistic policy. "Only from a height of 30,000 feet," in the words of former chairman Robert Reibestein. The Foundation Board consists on the one hand of top executives from the business world and from public administration who share a love of music, and on the other of representatives of the Association Board (members of the orchestra). The managing director and their deputies are always present at meetings, along with a constantly rotating member of the orchestra who has no formal management function. "The greatest danger for any management board is that a problem exists in the organization that we don't know about," says Louise Fresco, explaining this additional, informal representation. "We want to continue to hear suggestions at first hand from the orchestra members about how we can do things better."

The role of informal discussion is at least as important as that of the formal management structure. The managing director, for example, always consults the chairs of the Foundation Board, the Association Board and the Artistic Council when considering important events or making urgent decisions. The chief conductor is also closely involved, especially, of course, when it comes to artistic decisions, or when a member of the orchestra is not performing to expectations. In the latter case, informal channels will always be explored first in an attempt to speak with the musician in question and come to a solution.

All these committees, decision rights and consultation structures sound unnecessarily complicated, and yet the whole thing works very well. "This way of leading is more difficult than in a top-down structure," says former managing director Loot. "It's an awkward structure to work in, because the people whose boss you are are also your bosses, through the Association Board and the Foundation Board. Ultimately, everything works, because musicians and managers share the same goals. And the big advantage for the orchestra members involved in management is that they commit to the policy and explain it to the rest of the orchestra."

The consultative model of the RCO is therefore an important factor in the sense of responsibility that the orchestra members feel, as discussed in Chapter Three. "The many consultation bodies and the sense of shared responsibility for its leadership have protected the orchestra from the trade union mentality," writes Hans Ferwerda in his book *Bravo!* "Instead of an 'us and them' culture, we see a high level of shared responsibility, and many orchestra members take part in committees and consultative bodies in their often long careers. Over the years, the shared realization has grown that the artistic quality of the orchestra is linked very closely to the way the opinions of the musicians are taken seriously, and that flexibility is needed to take advantage of certain opportunities."[12] This flexibility works both ways. "As members of the Foundation Board, we are also constantly thinking about what our role is," says Louise Fresco. "We are always trying to establish a state of equilibrium where we can make a useful contribution though we are not, of course, looking to take over from the day-to-day management or the Artistic Council."

All this is in stark contrast to orchestras that do not have a comparable consultation structure. In the United States, orchestras are managed more as business corporations, even if they have a not-for-profit structure. Representation and power of individuals in the governing bodies show a direct correlation to their financial contribution. The leadership style is top-down, and the relationships between musicians and management are often antagonistic. Pamela Rosenberg, who was the intendant[13] of the Berlin Philharmonic Orchestra from 2006 to 2010, takes the appointment of the new chief conductor of the Los Angeles Philharmonic as an example: "When the members of the Berlin Philharmonic heard that their fellow musicians [in LA] were only informed at the press conference that Gustavo Dudamel was to be their new chief conductor, they were absolutely speechless. Not because they thought Dudamel was a bad choice – he is an excellent young conductor – but because of the fact that the musicians were entirely not involved in the decision."

In France, too, direct participation of the orchestra members in decision-making is less usual. "In the French orchestras you see a strong trade union mentality," says Loot, who spent some years as artistic director of the Orchestre National de France in Paris following his time with the Concertgebouw Orchestra. "For instance, the members of the orchestra

---

[12] Ferwerda (2013).

[13] In many European theatres and opera houses, the *Intendant* is a manager who has broad managerial control over various aspects of the company.

were forced to join the general strike against the raising of the retirement age, even though some of them did not want to do so. Management was also top down. Based on my RCO background, I tried a few times to start consultative talks with the members of the orchestra, but everybody found that highly unusual. On the other hand, I was sometimes expected to implement decisions made – without any prior consultation – by the management of Radio France, under whose aegis the orchestra fell. Sometimes the members of the orchestra were angry about a decision that had been made. In that case, they would hang a letter up in the canteen in which they would accuse the radio bosses of goodness knows what. I used to ask the managers if they were worried by it. But they would just shrug their shoulders as if to say: 'That's the way we do things round here'." It's very different way from that of the Concertgebouw Orchestra.

Solo trombonist van Rijen confirms this picture: "In France, it's the mayor or the Minister of Culture who decides who becomes chief conductor. As a result, they don't always choose the best conductor, or the conductor that is best suited to the orchestra – these are, after all, often political decisions. The imposition of policy is the reason why the musicians really regard playing in their orchestra as 'a job'. They put their creativity into the music they make in their small ensembles, not the music they make for the orchestra."

It is remarkable that the *Gramophone* list of the top 20 orchestras of the world does not contain a single French orchestra, although the country produces many great musicians and has a very rich musical tradition – Jean-Baptiste Lully, Jean-Philippe Rameau, Hector Berlioz, Camille Saint-Saëns, Georges Bizet, Gabriel Fauré, Claude Debussy, Maurice Ravel, Francis Poulenc, Olivier Messiaen, to name but a few leading French composers. Although other factors undoubtedly also play a role, such as the way French music courses are focused more on solo performance, it seems reasonable to consider that the absence of French orchestras in the top 20 has something to do with the lack of participative management by orchestra members. Self-determination thus seems to be an important factor in the success of top international orchestras. Van Rijen: "The top four orchestras on the *Gramophone* list – the Concertgebouw Orchestra, the Berlin Philharmonic, the Vienna Philharmonic and the London Symphony Orchestra – all allow their musicians a significant form of participative decision-making."

Successful companies, too, often have some form of participative decision-making. The participative democracy of Gore is an obvious example. But so is the partnership structure of the large strategic management consulting firms, where the partners choose their leader from their midst for a number of years. A much broader example is the system of *Mitbestimmung* or 'co-determination' in Germany, whereby almost half of the members of the board of any large company must consist of employee representatives. Scientific research has shown a positive effect of co-determination on workers' productivity.[14] Here, too, it is tempting to ascribe Germany's economic success at least in part to the sense of responsibility that people feel thanks to co-determination, if it leads to constructive dialogue, fewer strikes, greater commitment and wage moderation in times of economic hardship.

An interesting form of co-determination in the Netherlands is the cooperative, the legal form of companies such as FrieslandCampina, Univé and Rabobank. Former Shell boss and management researcher Arie de Geus describes how important the cooperative structure of Rabobank has been to its relative resilience in the current financial crisis: "The bank is successful due to its cooperative ownership structure, in which the members retain the upper hand. When, in the 1990s, a number of alpha males came to power and wanted to take the bank aggressively forward, their plans were thwarted by the farmers of Friesland and Brabant. Power there is not concentrated, but distributed among the members."[15] This is only possible, of course, if the system of co-determination has been properly institutionalized within the organization.

These checks and balances are similar to those we saw at the Concertgebouw Orchestra. In addition to the management bodies we have already discussed, the orchestra actually has two further lines of defence for maintaining the balance of power and guaranteeing the circle of iconic competence. The first is the sense of responsibility and leadership potential that every individual feels. Thanks to the way the orchestra is organized, there are many people who can take on a leading role. One example of a key function behind the scenes is the orchestra inspector, who forms an

---

[14] F.R. FitzRoy & K. Kraft (2005). 'Co-determination, Efficiency and Productivity'. *British Journal of Industrial Relations*, vol. 43, nr. 2, p. 233-247.

[15] P. Couwenbergh (2013). 'De financiële wereld heeft te veel Icarussen gekend. Dat heeft de crisis wel geleerd'. *fd.weekend*, 12 january.

important link between the concert podium and the administrative office. "He or she is partly responsible for the staff planning of the orchestra and for looking after the conductors and soloists," says editor Koopman. "Former orchestra inspector Theo Berkhout, who worked with Haitink for 25 years and with Chailly for 16 years, and who supported generations of orchestra members, played a significant role in professionalizing this vital function."

The other layer yet to be dealt with consists of the organizations surrounding the KCO, such as the Concertgebouw Donors' Foundation, the Association of Friends of the Concertgebouw and of the Royal Concertgebouw Orchestra, and Entrée, the Association of Young Audiences of the Concertgebouw Orchestra. "The donors and the Friends are real friends," says solo bassist Seldis. "I have never seen it work that way in an orchestra before. In other orchestras, I got the impression the donors were mainly there to give money. That's not the way it is here. Of course, the donations are important, but more than that, the donors are always sincerely interested in the orchestra, and even go on tour with us. A meeting with friends is always nice for the orchestra members." The donors are located not only in Amsterdam, but also in Belgium, France, Switzerland, the UK and the United States.

All these layers of responsibility make the virtuous circle of competence robust. As with Steinway, the quality DNA is deeply rooted, and helps the organization recover when things go wrong. In Chapter One we saw that the Concertgebouw Orchestra has had plenty of difficult moments in its history, but that it has always been able to rely on its virtuous circle of competence to bring it back on track. Only time will tell if Apple has enough distributed leadership to overcome the death of Steve Jobs in the long term. It will also become clear if there was any complementary leadership at all in Apple so that the organization can continue down the same successful path. In any case, in the Concertgebouw Orchestra everybody agrees that the governance structure, with its distributed leadership and extremely broadly shared sense of responsibility, forms an important explanation for the orchestra's long-term success. "The Concertgebouw Orchestra is like a house," Jansons says. "It doesn't fall down if you remove one brick."

# Social Cohesion

Before we began the research for this book, we already had an idea of which elements might make the Concertgebouw Orchestra and other icons successful, based on what we had heard, seen and read. In the course of our interviews and literature research, many of our ideas were confirmed, while others were debunked. And occasionally we came across something new that we had not thought of before. The stories told by orchestra members about the importance of the tours are a good example.

Solo trombonist van Rijen: "The tours are a huge boon for the atmosphere and spirit of cooperation in the orchestra. Petty irritations are much easier to resolve, because you are together a lot more on an informal basis. When you're traveling, you soon get to know each other. It always feels a bit like a youth orchestra – you always meet up for a beer after the concert. And the French members of the orchestra, for example, always make sure we have cheese and wine on the bus. Under those conditions, you soon iron out any underlying differences, and you gain a deeper understanding of your fellow players."

Cellist Tom: "On tour you get to see the other side of people. They broaden your horizons. And if there is any friction in the orchestra, it will surface when you're on tour."

Member of the Foundation Board Louise Fresco: "One of the board members almost always goes on tour. That's one of the best ways to understand what's going on in the orchestra."

Former chair of the Foundation Board Maarten van Veen: "I always went on tour at least twice a year with the orchestra, which was very important for social cohesion. My wife always accompanied me. She sometimes heard more than I did if one of the orchestra members had a problem. That was really helpful to me in solving problems in the orchestra."

And all of a sudden we saw a pattern: consultants often travel together for projects and training. The Shell expats spend years together cooped up in compounds, often on hardship postings. The Cirque du Soleil is always on the road. In restaurants, staff always stay for a drink afterwards. We realized that many iconic organizations develop social cohesion through team members being together outside of the work environment, and that this is an extra factor that strengthens the circle of iconic competence.

This social cohesion does not always have to come about through traveling – not every branch of industry requires being on the road. Pixar, instead, has an enormous central atrium where employees can meet very easily. To ensure that people really did congregate there, Steve Jobs had mailboxes, a café, meeting rooms, and a gift shop located around the atrium. And anyone who still doesn't want to use the atrium is forced to, because the only restrooms in the whole building can only be reached through the atrium. "In the beginning I thought it was a ridiculous plan," says Darla Anderson, executive producer for a number of Pixar films. "I need to use the bathroom every 30 minutes. I didn't want to walk all the way through the atrium every time. It was just a waste of time. But Steve said: "Everybody has to run into each other." He really believed that the best meetings happened by accident, in the hallway or parking lot. And do you know what? He was right. I get more done having a cup of coffee and striking up a conversation or walking to the bathroom and running into unexpected people than I do sitting at my desk."[16]

Steinway even had a whole village built to forge his employees into a closer team, and to retain their craftsmanship. Starting in 1870, Heinrich Engelhard Steinway built Steinway Village. It was not only the location to all the essential stages of the production process, such as a sawmill and an iron foundry, but also to houses for employees, a kindergarten, a library, and a number of parks.[17]

Social cohesion in organizations gets off to a good start due to their iconic status and the strict selection process that goes with it. The fact that few make it through the selection acts as a kind of onboarding process through which you suddenly feel part of the organization. In the words of one All Blacks captain who was asked how he felt when he was selected: "To be an All Black was every young rugby player's dream ... so it was a proud moment ... it was the biggest feeling on earth really."

# Common Thread

As part of our research, we call Dieter Flury, solo flutist and business manager of the Vienna Philharmonic, and we show him the circle of iconic competence. He does not hesitate to say that the circle perfectly summarizes the essence of the Vienna Philharmonic's success, and he explains the details of each element in his orchestra. What strikes us, however, is that while the parts of the circle at the Vienna Philharmonic are indeed the same, the way they are implemented differs from the Concertgebouw Orchestra. We hear the same story when we speak to Fergus McWilliam, second horn player and, until recently, chairman of the employee council at the Berlin Philharmonic. What we see is that for each individual orchestra, the virtuous circle is consistent: there is a common thread running through all the elements, which turns each of these orchestras into a unique group of people who each earn their place in their own way in the top three orchestras of the world.

The Berlin Philharmonic places more emphasis on the individual qualities of the musicians. We saw in Chapter Two that the salaries there are very good, and that the selection pressure remains high, even after the audition. In the Berlin Philharmonic, it is more common than in the Concertgebouw Orchestra for musicians to fail their trial period of one or two years. It is a competitive battle to retain only the very best musicians, and only those who can cope under the enormous pressure to perform.

This particular selection method also influences the kind of team the orchestra becomes. "An orchestra of soloists" is what Van Biemen calls the Berliner, where he spent two years as an academician. But it still remains "a family", says Pamela Rosenburg, former intendant of the orchestra. "Once people have been given a permanent contract, there is more understanding for any temporary quality problems, and we look for a solution." Even so, it seems that at the Berliner Philharmonic, the pressure that the musicians

---

[16] W. Isaacson (2011). Steve Jobs, New York: Simon and Schuster.

[17] A. Singer (1986). *Labor management relations at Steinway & Sons, 1853–1896.* New York: Garland.

feel to perform is driven more by *peer pressure*, whereas at the RCO it is driven more by group *trust*.

This team dynamic has its own consequences for the music that each orchestra produces. The Berliner Philharmonic is described in terms of 'lions in the arena', or 'scaling the mountain peaks'. Whereas the Concertgebouw Orchestra is famed for its chameleon-like ability to perform a broad repertoire of music in differing styles, the style of the Berlin Philharmonic is "very well suited to play a certain repertoire, but not for everything", in the words of Loot. "It's violence every night. That works very well for works by Richard Strauss or Wagner, and less for Mozart or an early Beethoven. But the Berlin Philharmonic has completely perfected the repertoire that is best suited to it, and its audiences know what to expect." If you go to hear Strauss's Alpine Symphony by the Berlin Philharmonic, then you know for sure it's going to be a flawless spectacle.

There are thus clear differences in the way the Berlin Philharmonic and the RCO interpret the virtuous circle, but the way the elements work is basically the same: the right people make a fantastic team which produces a unique result, which in turn attracts top people of the right calibre. The peripheral factors discussed in this chapter are also very similar. Like the Concertgebouw Orchestra, the Berlin Philharmonic is characterized by a high degree of self-management – the musicians have direct representation in the orchestra's day-to-day management. "There is a high degree of self-regulation," says Rosenberg. "It's been like that since the orchestra started. The orchestra decides for itself who will play when in the orchestra, and when in a chamber music ensemble. The musicians keep track of this by themselves. As intendant, I usually didn't know from one week to the next who would be playing."

The epitome of self-management is to be found at the Vienna Philharmonic. This orchestra is truly a self-regulating organization. The entire management consists of musicians, and the orchestra has not had a permanent conductor since 1933. One of the musicians is said to have replied, when asked by an acquaintance what the programme would be that evening under one of the guest conductors: "I don't know what he is conducting, but we're playing the Pastoral (Beethoven's Symphony No. 6)."[18]

Here, too, the orchestra culture begins with the selection process, which is very strongly focused on group dynamics. "The market for well-qualified musicians is very large," says Flury. "There is a wide choice of musicians with technical skills on the international market. But not of musicians with stylistic skills. And the chemistry has to be right; the musicians have to want to completely become one with the orchestra." He stresses the importance of the quality of *all* the orchestra members. "Our best-known quality is the warmth of our sound, especially of our strings. That sound is determined 90% by our tutti players. And the tutti are as strong as their weakest link. Compared with this, finding good soloists on the international market is actually easier."

The enormous amount of self-regulation in the orchestra is encouraged by the fact that the musicians of the Vienna Philharmonic always play in the State Opera. "We play 300 nights a year in operas," says Flury. "The conductor spends most of his time dealing with the singers and the stage, so the orchestra is used to a large degree of autonomy. That drives a high degree of musical self-management." No wonder, then, that leaders who do not show respect stand little chance of success at the Vienna Philharmonic – they simply will not be listened to. "I always let the orchestra play without me first, to see which way it is going," says the Indian conductor Zubin Mehta about how he deals with the Vienna Philharmonic.

It is good to see how everything works for these three leading orchestras. They have a very clear thread running through their people, the team and the timeless results. A thread which makes each of them unique in their own way, and which is in itself self-reinforcing: a certain kind of result is a powerful attraction to a certain type of musician to whom it is best suited. This can either be the high degree of openness and the chameleon-like ability of the RCO, or the emphasis on individual virtuosity and playing together in small groups which gives the Berlin Philharmonic the responsiveness and dynamic of a string quartet, or the attention given to stylistic fit and sound colour which makes the Vienna Philharmonic the orchestra with the warmest string sound and *Schmelz*[19].

If we look at the world's top management consulting firms, we also see differences between them. Just like orchestras, however, these companies share a common thread. Besides McKinsey, there are a few other management

---

[18]  Anecdote related by Bert Koopman in conversation with the authors.

[19]  Or melodiousness

consulting firms that are regarded as leaders in their field, are popular among graduates of top universities, and which provide good examples of circles of iconic competence, but differ in the interpretation they give to them.

The interpretation given to the virtuous circle at McKinsey can be traced back to the original ambition of James O. McKinsey and Marvin Bower to give *lawyer-like* advice of the very highest professionalism to the leaders of the most prestigious companies. Being part of – and strengthening – the networks of top executives is a fundamental part of this. The partners and directors of McKinsey are also to be found on all sorts of management and advisory boards. This extends to their own alumni network, the largest and best functioning of any strategic management consulting firm. The alumni network actually continues into the network of board members. Its origins are also reflected in the executive perspective that characterizes McKinsey in the advice it provides. For this reason, it is hardly surprising that McKinsey has delivered decisive contributions to making companies better managed over time, for example by making the Business Unit commonplace as a governance model.

The ambition to provide advice of the highest professional standard is also reflected in their circle of competence. Of course, being undisputed market leader and focusing on the most prestigious companies exerts an unequalled power of attraction on the most talented individuals. But talent development only really gets under way once the extremely stringent selection process has been completed. Pressure to perform, *up or out*, but also the support that is offered to get the most out of oneself creates a hothouse atmosphere for growing talent. McKinsey's origins are also expressed in the highly professional way in which it comes up with the right advice. First of all, the advice must be of the highest analytical quality in order to achieve the greatest possible objectivity. McKinsey outstrips all other consulting firms in its ability to deliver high quality advice with the greatest consistency. Moreover, the quality is consistent in all countries and offices.

To take another example, the circle of competence of leading consultant Bain & Company has a different thread running through it. Bain came into existence following a split with the more concept-driven Boston Consulting Group (BCG). Bill Bain, and the others who followed him from BCG, wanted to work longer and more closely with individual companies. They believed this would make it possible to work more extensively on the applicability of their recommendations for the companies they were working for and consequently to help in implementing the recommendations. To give strength to this approach, Bain would for a long time only work for one company exclusively in each branch of industry – in return, of course, for well-earned client loyalty. It is significant that on its web page Bain until recently included a chart showing how its clients were faring compared with the S&P 500 (according to this analysis, Bain clients did four times better than the index average in the period 1980 to 2013). Compared with other strategic management consulting firms, Bain has more private investors (private equity) among its clients. This kind of client fits perfectly with the total company perspective that drives Bain in its advice work, such as Bain's characteristic *full potential analysis*.

The idea of a common thread fits very nicely with the *activity system concept* familiar from business studies literature. This concept was popularized by the American Harvard Professor Michael Porter in his famous article *'What is Strategy?'*.[20] In this article, Porter argues that organizations that want to be successful in the long term need to define a few core activities that uniquely differentiate them from their competitors and which, between them, have a strong strategic fit. He takes Vanguard, the American investment firm, as an example: Vanguard "aligns all activities with its low-cost strategy … The company distributes its funds directly, avoiding commissions to brokers." Because the company is already very good in all its core activities, and because these activities reinforce one other, it is very hard for competitors to replicate the system as a whole. Companies with a properly functioning *activity system*, which they continue to improve, can therefore build and sustain a long-lasting edge over their competitors.

This works in exactly the same way for the common thread running through organizations – the fit of the elements in the circle of competence. The fact that these organizations have unique qualities in each of the elements of the circle, and the fact that these are mutually reinforcing, is the reason why their iconicity is very difficult for others to replicate, let alone surpass. That is true at least as long as they continue to improve themselves and to adapt, following the common thread that makes them unique. The RCO is well aware of this. In the words of Van Rijen: "We must not try to become the Berlin Philharmonic."

---

[20] M.E. Porter (1996). 'What is Strategy?' *Harvard Business Review*, Nov-Dec.

# CHAPTER 6
# HOW THE VIRTUOUS CIRCLE BEGINS

The "Big Four" of Johns Hopkins Medicine in 1906:
They had been attracted by the Hopkins trustees as young
and brilliant physicians and they redefined surgery and
medical teaching in the United States.

This chapter addresses the question of
how the virtuous circle can be set in motion,
both in new and existing organizations.
Most of the iconic organizations seem to have
evolved from a visionary, complementary
leader who was able to attract a group of top
people. However, in order to retain the circle
of competence after the departure of such a
leader, it is crucial that sufficient substance
has been built up in the other elements of
the circle from the start.

Up till now we have looked only at how iconic organizations keep their virtuous circle going. Because it is a circle, the constituent parts impact one other, and this has a self-reinforcing effect. This gives the circle enormous resilience, but it also raises the question: where does the circle begin? How, for example, do you find the right people, if you do not yet have the iconic status to attract them? And how do you then get the wheels turning to achieve iconic status? That is what this chapter is about.

In this chapter, too, we have again sought to identify the characteristic similarities between the iconic organizations we have studied – similarities that we do see in budding icons, but not in most other organizations. In general, we see roughly three phases on the ascent to iconic status.

In Phase One , the *visionary leaders phase*, the virtuous circle is set in motion. One method seems to dominate here. One or more visionary leaders succeed in creating such a tangible vision of the unparalleled results that they aspire to, that they can then use it to attract the talent they need to start achieving actual results.

Next follows Phase Two, *implementing the circle of iconic competence*. Once the first unparalleled results have been achieved, it is important to make sure the organization can sustain them. This means that all elements of the virtuous circle must be realized. This is often the moment the organzsation breaks free from its original visionary leaders and transitions into complementary and distributed leadership.

Finally, in Phase Three, comes *iconic competence*. Achieving unparalleled results is not the same as being iconic. Anyone can produce results, but iconicity can only be *ascribed* to you. The most important difference between the two is time: if you continue to produce unparalleled results for longer than anyone actually believes possible, then you are laying the foundations for iconicity.

If an organization achieves this, the circle of competence will be considerably more robust. Iconic organizations show exceptional resilience that enables them to withstand and recover from occasional difficult periods of suboptimal leadership.

In this chapter we shall go into the three phases in more detail. We shall begin with a wonderful illustration of Phase One, an article published 120 years ago by a Dutch newspaper, the *Algemeen Handelsblad*. It is almost beyond belief that the most important characteristics that would ultimately make the Concertgebouw Orchestra world famous were essentially already present – and how clearly the newspaper editor could see that at the time.

# Fifth Anniversary

*So, the fifth anniversary of the founding of the Concertgebouw is already behind us. In normal life, the completion of a period of five years is not normally a cause for celebration, except, perhaps, in the student world, but it is nevertheless commendable that in the case of the Concertgebouw, convention has been broken and the start of a new period of five years has been marked with some honour. For an art institution such as the Concertgebouw, the first five years are, after all, of overriding importance.*

*These five years were a period of struggle, through which the foundation has had to fight its way. If it had not succeeded in winning a place in the hearts and minds of the populace, then, alas, the chance that it would ever have made its tenth anniversary would have been small. We all know how the Concertgebouw has fared. The institution has not been spared its days of struggle, although it has been able to withstand them and in this time the Concertgebouw has become an essential factor in the musical life of the capital.*

*This is first and foremost down to the leader of the orchestra, Willem Kes, that serious musician, conscious of his noble calling not to entertain audiences, but to allow them to enjoy, and also to teach them to enjoy the best and noblest of what the noble art of music has brought forth. In all of this, teaching the public was not the easiest part of the task.*

*It was not so long ago that audiences regarded a concert as a welcome opportunity to meet up with friends; to come and go as they pleased, without any regard for the orchestra; and to chatter and joke while waiters rushed back and forth, while the orchestra was playing. If I may say a word in the audiences' defence, it is that the orchestral directors were not always interested in entertaining their listeners. They had a relatively limited number of repertoire pieces – symphonies and overtures – which they reeled off with the complacency that comes from routine, and neither side – audience or orchestra – complained about the other. Only one small clique was not party to this state of affairs; they formed, among other things, the core of those who attended the concerts given by Wedemeyer's Orchestra Association, and they were among the first members of the Concertgebouw.*

*It was then that Kes put an end to everything that smacked of habit and routine, both in the orchestra and among the members of the audience. The waiters were shooed away, and the audience awed into breathless silence, because he would not begin until it was so quiet you could hear a pin drop, and would even tap his baton if anyone had the audacity to break his concentration by walking to their place in creaking boots.*

*In this way, Kes forced people to listen, but more importantly he awakened people's interest by breathing new life into the old, tried and tested beauty, and by reading us an anthology of the many new developments in orchestral music. There was no question of monotony here. Beethoven, Bach, Wagner, Brahms, Liszt, Berlioz, St.-Saëns, Dvorak, Haydn, d'Indy and so many others appeared in a colourful variety of programmes, and they were all accorded the interpretation of which they are worthy.*

*However, Kes is not the only one who deserves to be honoured, because the members of the orchestra, many of whom have been there the full five years, also have a right to praise. They feel that their orchestra, of which they are part, has a name to uphold, and under the spirited leadership of the conductor they give their utmost, in full knowledge that not a single detail escapes his attention. This is what has made the Concertgebouw Orchestra the best in our country, and one of the best in Europe, unsurpassed either in its interpretation of a symphony by Brahms or Beethoven, or in a symphonic poem of Liszt, Berlioz or d'Indy, unsurpassed also in the art of accompanying a soloist – just ask the artists who have played in the Concertgebouw!*

*Algemeen Handelsblad, 5 November 1893*

N°. 1.                                                                    Prijs 10 . Cents.

NAAMLOOZE VENNOOTSCHAP „HET CONCERTGEBOUW"
HOUBRAKENSTRAAT.

*Zaterdag 3 November 1888 – 8 ure*

tot opening van het eerste Abonnementsjaar

# PHILHARMONISCH CONCERT

*onder leiding van den Heer W. KES.*

1. **Ouverture** „Zur Weihe des Hauses", op. 124.

   Componirt im Jahre 1822 zur Eröffnung des Josephstädter
   Theaters in Wien, von . . . . . . . . . . . . . . L. VAN BEETHOVEN.

2. **Variationen** über ein Thema von J. HAYDN, op. 56ª, von . . . J. BRAHMS.

3. **Phaéton.** Poéme symphonique, op. 39 . . . . . . . . . . CAMILLE SAINT-SAËNS.

   NOTICE. — Phaéton a obtenu de conduire dans le ciel le char du Soleil son
   père. Mais ses mains inhabiles égarent les coursiers. Le char flamboyant, jeté
   hors de sa route, s'approche des régions terrestres. Tout l'univers va périr
   embrassé, lorsque Jupiter frappe de sa foudre l'imprudent Phaéton

4. **Vorspiel** zu den „Meistersingern von Nürnberg". . . . . . . . R. WAGNER.

5. **Sinfonie** N°. 3 (Irische) F-moll, op. 28 (Eerste uitvoering hier te lande.) CH. VILLIERS STANFORD.

   1. Allegro moderato.              3. Andante con moto.
   2. Allegro molto vivace.          4. Allegro moderato, ma con fuoco.

*Zondag 4 November 1888, des middags te 2 ure*

MATINÉE MUSICALE.

Newspaper ad publicizing the first concert of the Concertgebouw Orchestra.
3 November 1888

# Phase One: Visionary leaders

The article in the *Handelsblad* shows how underdeveloped the classical music scene in Amsterdam was before the arrival of the Concertgebouw Orchestra. "Lovely people, but poor musicians," Johannes Brahms noted. Nor was there really a suitable hall in which the large-scale symphonic repertoire could be performed. At the end of 1881, six prominent Amsterdam citizens, all of whom shared a love for music, decided enough was enough. They wanted to build a concert hall in the spirit of the Tonhalle in Düsseldorf, and set up a new orchestra that deserved to play in it.[1]

The project launched by these six gentlemen nearly failed on a number of occasions. For one, there were problems with the city council in identifying a suitable piece of land, and the amount of capital needed could not initially be found. After several rounds of financing involving the issuing of stock and bonds, construction could finally begin. The budget was exceeded and refinancing needed on several occasions, but the Concertgebouw was finally inaugurated on 11 April 1888, though not yet with its own orchestra, which was yet to be formed.[2]

To form the orchestra, 32-year-old Willem Kes was appointed the first conductor of the Concertgebouw on 1 September 1888. Prior to this, Kes had been the conductor of a choir and orchestra in Dordrecht, and had already earned some national and international fame as a solo violinist. In his first months, he succeeded in gathering together an orchestra of 65 people, all of whom met his requirements. Despite limited time, Kes had all the musicians audition, and maintained a minimum level of proficiency that they were all expected to reach. If he could not find anyone good enough, he looked abroad – all very innovative for the Amsterdam music scene. Furthermore, he rehearsed the programmes much more intensively than was usual in those days.[3]

Because Kes from the first moment refused to make any concessions on the quality of the musicians and the commitment he expected from them, audiences were immediately enthusiastic. *Caecilia*, a music magazine of the period, praised the "noble full-bodied sound" of the first concert on 3 November 1888. "With an orchestra such as this, under the leadership of such a thorough and meticulous mind, the members of the Concertgebouw – as yet too limited in number – can expect many a moment of great and true enjoyment of art." Prophetic words.[4]

It is fascinating to see how the seeds of the circle of competence had been planted at the orchestra's founding, and within five years had grown to their first blossoming, as is clear from the article in the *Algemeen Handelsblad*. Attracting and selecting the right people, the demands placed on their skill level and commitment, the extensive rehearsals, the striking of the right balance between a familiar and a new repertoire, and the drive to become ever better – all of this was there from the very beginning. The vision that the founding fathers and Willem Kes had to radically improve the standard of music in Amsterdam laid the foundation for an orchestra that would be among the best in the world.

Just like the Concertgebouw Orchestra, other icons were also founded by one or two founding fathers who had a very clear vision of a transformational improvement and who gathered together a group of talented people to turn that vision into reality. This was often at the foundation of the organization, but sometimes the will to truly transform an industry or competency came only later, as for example with elBulli or Shell (about which we will say more in Chapter Seven). A good example of an organization in which the right people with a transformational vision were present at the start, as they were with the RCO, is the Johns Hopkins University School of Medicine in the US state of Maryland.

The institute is regarded as providing one of the best medical university educations in the United States, and is able to attract the highest research funds in the country. The teaching hospital that is attached to it has been consistently rated America's best; from 1991 to 2011 it came first every single year in the annual *U.S. News and World Report* on hospitals in the United States. The institute was founded with the help of a bequest from railroad tycoon Johns Hopkins, who wanted it used to build a hospital that would "compare favourably with any other institution of like character in this country or in Europe". He appointed 12 prominent Baltimore

---

[1]  J. Giskes (1989a). 'Opbouw (1881-1888)' (p. 14). In: van Royen et al. (1989).

[2]  Giskes (1989a).

[3]  Giskes (1989b).

[4]  Giskes (1989b).

citizens as trustees responsible for realizing his dream, and urged them to "secure for the service of the hospital physicians and surgeons of the highest character and greatest skill". Most importantly, Hopkins told the trustees they should "bear constantly in mind that it is my wish and purpose that the hospital shall ultimately form a part of the Medical School of that university for which I have made ample provision in my will".[5] On his death in 1873, he bequeathed $7 million, at the time the greatest philanthropical bequest ever made.

The combination of university and hospital that Hopkins sought to create sounds like a logical choice to us, but at the time it represented a radical departure from the model that was usual in America. Back then, doctors often had no more than a secondary education, followed by a two- or three-year medical degree with little or no clinical practice.[6] Doctors could set up their own practice without ever having touched a patient. Academic teaching hospitals did not exist in the United States.

Johns Hopkins changed this system completely, and took the German model with its much higher scientific standards as a starting point. First, four young doctors of the highest calibre were recruited by offering them attractive research opportunities. Next, candidates who wished to apply for a university place were required to have higher qualifications in chemistry, physics and biology, and were subjected to strict entrance exams. The teaching at Johns Hopkins emphasized the scientific method, and was linked to both laboratory work and patient clinical practice, working closely with the teaching hospital. Finally, the new model offered scope for further specialization, and for the creation of the first post-doctoral internships.

Furthermore, Johns Hopkins precipitated a revolution in surgery by paying attention to sterility and by introducing the wearing of rubber gloves during operations. Operative and life-saving treatments for breast cancer, hernias and gastro-intestinal disorders were first carried out here.

---

[5] A. McGehee Harvey & V.A. McKusick (1989). *A Model of Its Kind: Volume 1 – A Centennial History of Medicine at Johns Hopkins.* Baltimore: Johns Hopkins University Press.

[6] Johns Hopkins website, http://www.hopkinsmedicine.org/about/history/, accessed on 5 April 2013.

[7] Johns Hopkins website, http://web.jhu.edu/aroundtheworld, accessed on 17 March 2013.

Library of the Johns Hopkins University

The success of Johns Hopkins did not go unnoticed. In a study that would ultimately revolutionize the whole of the American medical system, Abraham Flexner researched the 150 medical schools in the United States and Canada. Flexner found that only five of these were up to standard, and he named Johns Hopkins as exemplary among them. "The influence of this new foundation can hardly be overstated," he wrote. "It has finally cleared up the problem of standards and ideals, and its graduates have gone forth in small bands to found new establishments." The medical schools at the universities of Washington, Vanderbilt, Iowa, Duke and Rochester were directly modelled on Hopkins. Moreover, Johns Hopkins has produced 18 Nobel Prize winners, and currently has sister institutions following the same model across the world, including in China, Singapore and Italy.[7]

The parallels between Johns Hopkins and the Concertgebouw Orchestra are unmistakable: a small group of people, who have a dream of transforming the possible in their industry, apply rigorous selection methods to recruit a top team who can turn their vision into reality. In the same way, we saw how James McKinsey and Marvin Bower founded the consulting industry in its present form. Or how a small group of street artists breathed new life into the idea of a circus with Cirque du Soleil. Or how Heinrich Steinway and his sons made the piano into the instrument we hear today in the concert halls around the world.

However, you don't only need an inspiring vision and good people. You also need the right circumstances – and not every good idea grows into an icon. But what we do see is that the founders of icons have often given fate a helping hand, and remained extremely tenacious when fate didn't go their way. For example, the acoustics of the Concertgebouw are often mentioned as being essential to the quality of the RCO. These acoustics are a combination of good preparation (such as the use of blueprints from other good concert halls), tenacity (overcoming setbacks in the building and later rebuilding to improve the acoustics still further)[8] and a little luck (it was not entirely possible at the time to predict the qualities of a concert hall). In the spirit of Seneca: "Luck is what happens when preparation meets opportunity."

## Phase Two. Implementing the Circle of Competence

After the first notable successes of a budding icon, it becomes easier to recruit more good people, who in turn can strengthen the team and enable it to deliver even higher levels of quality – and so the virtuous circle of competence begins to take effect. Although initial fame often comes quite quickly, decades can often pass before the organization is classed as an undisputed icon. During this time the details of the circle of competence are filled in with ever-greater accuracy. The most difficult part of this is establishing distributed leadership and anchoring the circle in the entire organization. This is because, as we have already seen, an icon almost always begins with one or more visionary leaders. This creates inherent tension, because visionary leaders are not always the kind of people who strive for complementary or distributed leadership. Iconic organizations often go through a kind of emancipation or crisis, during which their dependence on one or more visionary leaders is diminished. There will come a time when the organization will have to go on without its founders, and it is then crucial that its leadership is sufficiently devolved and that the DNA of absolute aspiration is sufficiently anchored in the whole organization.

The example of the Harlem Globetrotters below shows clearly how an authoritarian leader can ultimately bring his icon into decline – but also how the DNA can later help the team come back to life.

In Chicago in 1926, a British Jew named Abe Saperstein, who came from a family of tailors, set up a team of talented basketball players who, because of their skin colour, were excluded from playing in official competitions. After a number of successful matches against local clubs in and around Chicago, Saperstein christened his team the Harlem Globetrotters, to emphasize the fact that they were a team of black players, and to create an air of exoticism (it would be another 40 years before the Globetrotters actually played a match in the famed New York neighbourhood).[9]

The Globetrotters played much better than their local – white – opponents, and the spectacular results they sometimes achieved were not always taken in the spirit of good sportsmanship. For this reason, they soon added an element of entertainment to their games: they played tricks with the ball, ran circles round their opponents and made spectacular throws towards the basket. In this way, the scores remained more modest and the white teams were spared too much ridicule. The combination of high-quality play and entertainment appealed to audiences, and the Globetrotters' star was soon in the ascendant. In its glory days, the club had four complete teams to choose from, which traveled around the United States and the rest of the world, playing hundreds of games a year. Venues were consistently sold out, something that the national competition the BAA (the forerunner of the NBA) was not usually able to do.

The Globetrotters achieved their finest hour in 1948, when the team played against the BAA champions the Minneapolis Lakers. In the run-up, the Lakers did not take the game too seriously – after all, they were the reigning champions, playing against what in their eyes was little more than a show team. However, the Globetrotters proved to be really good players and it turned into an unusually exciting match. At the halfway mark, the Lakers still had a comfortable lead of 32 to 23, but with only

[8]   J. Giskes (1989a), p. 24.
[9]   Harlem globetrotters website, http://www.harlemglobetrotters.com/history, accessed on 21 February 2013.

a minute to go before the whistle, their opponents closed the gap, with 59-59 on the scoreboard. The Globetrotters went in for a final attack, and in a blood-chilling moment the ball landed in the net, after the final buzzer had gone. But the referee decided that the throw was made before the bell, and in basketball that is what counts. The Globetrotters won with 61-59, and the 59,000-strong crowd – both black and white – went crazy. The black basketball team had written history.[10]

Ironically enough, the resounding success against the Lakers also marked the start of a long, slow decline for the Globetrotters. This is because the match revealed the enormous potential of black basketball players to the team managers in the national competition. At the start of the 1950s, the first black player was admitted to what would later become the NBA. Until that time, the Globetrotters' coach Saperstein had been able to get away with paying excessively low wages and an authoritarian leadership style: anyone who complained about the money or the management's inability to listen was soon shown the door, because there were always plenty of other talented black players with nowhere else to go. This all changed in the 1950s, when black players no longer had to make do with $4,000 a year with the Globetrotters, but could earn as much as $20,000 with an NBA team.

Despite this, the Globetrotters managed to reinvent themselves completely, focusing exclusively on playing show games against teams who everybody knew would lose. As the years went by, they set increasingly higher standards with shows that combined basketball and entertainment. A number of Hollywood films were made about the legendary team,[11] and the Globetrotters even had an extremely popular cartoon series. However, history repeated itself. The team's broad entertainment success began to turn against the players. After Saperstein's sudden death in 1968, the team was pushed slowly but surely to the margins.

"By 1993 the Globetrotters were simply not relevant any more," wrote former Globetrotter Mannie Jackson in the *Harvard Business Review*. "They weren't stylish, and they weren't cool. They weren't a priority for anyone." Jackson decided to take over the team and thus became the first black owner of a major sports team. "I had intended to tell them that we would be folding the team," he said, writing about his first speech. "But as I got into the speech and looked into the eyes of some of the great ones from the team's past, I started telling a different story. You know how sometimes ideas just come through you, and you start talking without a script? That's what happened to me. I started talking about building a competitive team, being known for our contributions to charity, being good to kids, and rebuilding the quality of the organization."

Jackson attracted really good players again and in this way built a team that really could win without having to agree the outcome before the match. His experience as a former executive of Honeywell enabled him to get the support organization quickly up to par. He fired those who did not perform or who could not adapt to the top level the team once again strove to reach. And most importantly of all, he brought the "wow" effect back into the games, with players who were highly skilled, and who could literally score with their eyes closed. By regularly playing against top teams, and winning, the Globetrotters found themselves being taken seriously again as a basketball team. Furthermore, the demonstration games were overhauled. These offered really competitive basketball once again, an amazing box of basketball tricks, and serious entertainment, including stand-up comedy. The whole thing was delivered with the choreography of a Broadway musical.

In the space of eight years, Jackson increased ticket receipts sixfold to $2 million, and turned a $1 million loss into a $9 million profit. The Globetrotters traveled the world once again, stunning audiences with their tricks and making them laugh at the same time. Nowadays, the scoreboard stands at 24,000 matches won, with only 345 lost, and the number is still rising.[12]

The Globetrotters are yet another example of how disastrous authoritarian leadership can be for an organization, and at the same time how powerful iconicity is in helping to get an organization back on top. We saw something similar in Chapter Four with Steinway, which managed to come back from a difficult period of almost 20 years to restore the glory of its concert grand pianos.

---

[10] http://www.mmbolding.com/basketball/Globetrotters.htm, opgehaald op 17 maart 2013.

[11] The History Channel. *Biography, The Harlem Globetrotters,* https://www.youtube.com/watch?v=SA8xF_zz1g8, opgehaald op 17 maart 2013.

[12] http://www.harlemglobetrotters.com/news/globetrotters-victorious-ice, opgehaald op 17 maart 2013.

Even the Concertgebouw Orchestra as an organization has been through good times and bad, and experienced a long evolution before it arrived at the current well-balanced leadership structure that we discussed in the previous chapter. When, after seven years, the orchestra was no longer able to keep the rising star Kes to itself, another promising music director was found in 1895 in the form of Willem Mengelberg. During his 50 years as a conductor, Mengelberg formed the promising ensemble into one of the best orchestras in the world and brought many famous composers, soloists and fellow conductors to Amsterdam – legends such as Gustav Mahler and Richard Strauss conducted and presented their works through the RCO. Mengelberg turned the orchestra into an icon of the music world. However, his authoritarian and confrontational leadership style also regularly led to conflicts – as we have seen in previous chapters – and earned him the nickname of "the little corporal". It was troubles with Mengelberg that led the members of the orchestra to set up the Concertgebouw Orchestra Association in 1915. Later conflicts also led to important leadership changes. Following a huge row in 1951 in which the Concertgebouw organization fired 62 members of the orchestra, the Netherlands Orchestra Foundation was finally founded, separating the orchestra from the concert hall in managerial and financial terms. Following several problems and changes of director in the 1980s and 1990s, the roles of artistic director and commercial director were combined into a single general director. The current checks and balances at the RCO have a long history, and the process of finding a good and workable structure was not without its many pitfalls.

Just like the RCO, Steinway, W.L. Gore, McKinsey, the Vienna and the Berlin Philharmonic were also able to turn initial successes into sustainable iconic organizations that were no longer dependent on one or a few visionary individuals. The question is what will happen to organizations that have reached almost iconic status in just one leadership generation. Will Apple and Pixar succeed in keeping their top status without Jobs? Or will a rising star like the Budapest Festival Orchestra (the ninth place on the *Gramophone* list and the only "young" orchestra)[13] succeed without its founder and conductor Ivan Fischer?

# Phase Three. Iconic Competence

At some point, the visionary leader(s) that created the organization leave. This moment heralds the third and decisive phase, as now the organization has to prove it has deeply internalized the absolute aspiration of its founders. Organizations that can keep the circle of iconic competence going, even after the departure of these first generation leaders, usually find it easier to remain iconic afterwards. But while even icons are not immune to disaster (think of Kodak), they appear surprisingly resilient in overcoming it. "Iconic status brings you recognition and a sense of security," says Fergus McWilliam of the Berlin Philharmonic. "That sense of security allows you to concentrate on performing to the best of your ability."

In the preceding chapters we discussed how iconic organizations can hold on to their success in Phase Three. The most important priority that comes out of this is a constant striving to improve people, the team, and results. "Less privileged orchestras remember the one or two concerts that were magical," says McWilliam. "Top orchestras remember that one concert that didn't go so well."

As the RCO, the All Blacks and others all show, iconic status can be held on to for a very long time – provided the organization shows unwavering commitment and continues to work at producing unparalleled results. Due to circumstances, however, an organization can get distracted and lower its level of absolute aspiration – for example, if financial performance gains the upper hand. Circumstances can also change, sometimes suddenly, so that unparalleled results are no longer within reach of the organization. But as we shall see in the next chapter, only in very rare cases does this lead to a definite demise of iconic organizations. As the former Shell CEO Jeroen van der Veer observed: "A circle of iconic competence is difficult to demolish!"

---

[13] The Budapest Festival Orchestra was founded by Ivan Fischer and Zoltan Kocsis in 1983, and is by far the youngest orchestra in *Gramophone* magazine's list of the world's top ten orchestras (see Chapter One).

# CHAPTER 7
# ICONS OF INDUSTRY

A storage tank for ammoniac from Shell in 1964

This chapter is about icons in the business world. How do the most successful companies become iconic in their primary competency domains? How do they make sure that their managers maintain their focus on results rather than on internal politics? Can the circle of iconic competence also work in companies with tens of thousands of employees? We shall discuss these questions using two case studies: one of the world's largest publicly listed companies (Shell) and one of the best performing conglomerates (Danaher).

Many of the icons that we have discussed up till now are relatively focused organizations, with one clear core competency. The majority of people in these organizations are directly involved in the core competency (the musicians in the Royal Concertgebouw Orchestra, the chefs at elBulli, the consultants at McKinsey), while the others play a supporting role in allowing the core competency to come to complete fruition.

Large companies, on the other hand, can have tens of thousands of employees, spread over a large variety of departments, production facilities and countries, all with their own competencies that are necessary for the success of the company. In these cases, it is not immediately clear how the circle of competence in this kind of company can work, if there is no obvious single competency to which it can be applied. Can a company with 10,000 employees grow into an icon in the same way as an orchestra with less than 200?

There is of course no fundamental reason why larger companies cannot be iconic. Even they can achieve the extraordinary level of performance for long enough to give them iconic status. This status will probably relate to an overarching competency, or indeed to a part of the competencies of the organization. It is possible for a company to be exemplary in a number of competencies. And in some cases, it is the company's products and services that will be accorded iconic status, such as the Gore-Tex™ membrane or Rolls-Royce cars.

We are going to answer this question by looking at two main examples: the number one company in the Fortune Global 500 in 2012,[1] and one of the best-performing conglomerates of the past few decades.

## Shell: Pushing the Envelope in Oil and Gas Exploration and Production

In 1890, a group of Dutch bankers, businessmen, and former colonial officials founded the Royal Dutch Company for the Exploitation of Petroleum Sources in Dutch East India, with the aim of exploiting oil reserves on Sumatra.[2] The company quickly grew with the discovery of new reserves of oil, building pipelines and refineries, and set up a sales organization.

In 1907 the company carried out a de facto merger with the Shell Transport and Trading Company,[3] another pioneer in the oil industry that, a few years earlier, had brought into service the world's first oil tanker, the Murex. As a unified force, the Royal/Shell Group was much better able to compete with the mighty Standard Oil, owned by Rockefeller, the American oil magnate. The merger would create a company with an unceasing aspiration to produce oil and gas under ever more challenging conditions and from ever more remote places anywhere in the world. The company would eventually grow into the world's largest public company, measured by revenues.[4] Former CEO Jeroen van der Veer reflected a century later: "Shell has always sought to experiment and push the boundaries."

The list of leading innovations that this desire to experiment has produced is long. For instance, in 1920 Shell was the first to chart underground structures and identify probable oil reserves using 2D seismic technology. In 1947, the company pumped the first commercial off-shore oil in the Gulf of Mexico – within the space of a few years Shell placed hundreds of oil wells there. In 1964, the company played an important role in developing techniques to liquefy gas, and to transport it overseas (even today, Shell still plays a leading role in the developments surrounding this Liquefied Natural Gas, or LNG). In the 1970s, Shell was one of the first to develop the oil fields under the North Sea, which are difficult to exploit because of their offshore location, the instability of the seabed, and the unpredictable weather. In the late 1970s, Shell made further innovations in offshore techniques, such as cost-efficient floating production, storage and dispatch installations for smaller oil fields, and with platforms, which for the first time could produce oil from reserves under more than 300 metres of water. In the 1980s, the company even drilled in water depths of 2.3 kilometres in the Gulf of Mexico, a new record. Furthermore, the company played a pioneering role at that time with 3D seismology and using supercomputers to make more accurate assessments of oil and gas reserves.

[1] *Fortune* (2012). 'Global 500', http://money.cnn.com/magazines/fortune/global500/2012/snap-shots/6388.html?iid=splwinners, accessed on 17 March 2013.

[2] *Encyclopaedia Britannica*, http://www.britannica.com/EBchecked/topic/511369/Royal-Dutch-Shell-PLC, accessed on 28 February 2013.

[3] In purely legal terms, the merger was not completed until 2005, with the formation of the publicly listed company Royal Dutch Shell plc.

[4] In 2012; see *Fortune* (2012).

With its successful completion of multi-billion dollar projects, which involve huge technical, infrastructural and political challenges, Shell belongs to the very best in its field. Finally – despite the occasional criticism in the media – the safety standards the company maintains all over the world are of the highest order, in many cases higher than local laws and regulations require.

Shell is not only a pioneer in the exploration and production of oil, but also in recruiting and training the engineers and managers who make it all possible. Thanks to its iconic competence, Shell exerts a powerful attraction as an employer of top engineers from such institutions as the Delft University of Technology and Imperial College London, and since the 1960s Shell has actively recruited all over the world. In order to select the right people, the company was one of the first to use assessment centres, choosing not only on technical ability, but also on leadership potential – by Shell managers (and not, therefore, by external agencies). The use of assessment centres is a practice that has since then been adopted by many other companies. "Selection is actually very simple," says van der Veer, "you look for people who are good at what they do, who can cope with extra responsibilities in parallel, and who at the same time can think about why their contribution fits into the bigger picture. These are people who want to carry on learning, who want to grow and be proud of what they do and who will act accordingly. This in fact applies to everyone in Shell; it is part of what makes Shell what it is. For example, like at the RCO, the service staff at Shell are just as proud of their company as the engineers. Some of them even buy shares in the company when they retire, just so they can continue to attend the shareholder meetings where they used to be present as service staff."

However, in the 1990s a subtle shift occurred. Up until that time, the only thing the people of Shell ever talked about was the latest record depth to which they had drilled under the sea, or how the company had managed to produce and transport gas under the most hostile conditions. Of course they had to make a profit, but that seemed to be more of a natural byproduct of pushing the boundaries of oil and gas exploration and production. But slowly, the emphasis shifted to financial targets, as growth, profit, return on equity and shareholder value became increasingly important. A clear illustration of this can be found in the tone of the annual reports from that time. "Our objective is to deliver the profitable growth which will provide the basis for continuing improvement in the return to our shareholder" is how the foreword to the 1997 annual report begins. This could just as easily have been the opening line for any other publicly listed company. Likewise, the rest of the foreword makes virtually no mention of the unique competencies in exploration and production that had helped make Shell great and its employees so proud. It is almost completely about capital expenditure, efficiency, growth, profit, stock levels, oil reserves, competitiveness, and cost reduction. Shell's absolute aspiration to overcome the biggest challenges in oil and gas exploration and production was slowly being compromised.

And so Shell was forced to work more quickly, employees were judged more and more on hard, short-term results, the bonus component of their salaries was increased and coupled mainly to financial goals, and people in leadership positions changed roles ever more frequently. "By the end of the 1990s, the average time in role at a leadership level had become too short," says Van der Veer. "This opened the door to planners who were never confronted with the consequences of their plans, and ultimately to *me-first* behaviour instead of the *company-first* mentality that we had seen up until that time." Looking back, it seems almost inevitable that things would go wrong.

And just how wrong they went! "I am becoming sick and tired about lying about the extent of our reserves issues and the downward revisions that need to be done because of far too aggressive/optimistic bookings." This is how an email begins from the former director of exploration Walter van de Vijver to the chairman of the board Sir Philips Watts, written on 9 November 2003.[5] The message leaked out into the media and led ultimately to the Shell oil reserve scandal. The proven oil reserves had to be revised down by almost 20%. In a settlement, Shell was forced to pay huge fines to the SEC, the American financial watchdog, and the value of the company on the stock exchange fell by many billions – the ironic result of a strategy that was supposed to be focused on shareholder value.

---

[5]   T. Macalister (2004). 'Shell admits it misled investors'. *The Guardian*, 20 April.

Shell design of the first floating plant for liquefied natural gas in the world, six times heavier than the largest aircraft carrier

The company licked its wounds and returned to the circle of compentence of old. "We brought back the average time in leadership roles to between four to eight years," says Van der Veer. "That is long enough. Make it any longer, and you risk getting too self-satisfied; make it any shorter, and you don't have time to achieve anything – and you can't judge if someone is really making a significant contribution." Engineers can once again be proud of the first offshore gas production platform to work on wind and solar energy (in 2006) or of the Sakhalin-II-LNG factory, the first in such difficult, cold circumstances (in 2009). In his foreword to the 2011 annual report, the CEO mentions in the very first paragraph the projects in which Shell has made a difference: Pearl GTL, Qatargas 4, and the extension of the Athabasca Oil Sands Project. Furthermore, he writes that "growth is a key part of our strategy, but so are operational excellence and the cultivation of future opportunities". And in 2012, Shell topped the Fortune 500 list of the world's greatest publicly listed companies.

# Iconic Competence Within a Large Company

The way the circle of iconic competence actually works at Shell is surprisingly similar to the way it works at the RCO. "This kind of virtuous circle has probably been working at Shell since 1930," says Van der Veer. "Not designed as such, but naturally developed. It is still largely responsible for Shell's success." Because of the enormous power of attraction exerted by the most advanced oil and gas company in the world, Shell can select the best people, give them extensive growth and training opportunities and form a top team that works at continuously improving the techniques it needs to find oil and gas and bring them to the surface. Everyone in the industry agrees that Shell is iconic in its primary competency, which is overcoming challenges in oil and gas exploration and production. And just like at the RCO, the virtuous circle that makes this iconic competency has a positive effect on the rest of the organization – even the non-engineers are proud of the company's technological successes.

There is a very clear common thread that runs through Shell's people, team and results, and which reaches even further, into the market segment within which the company operates. Given Shell's specific competency, it should come as no great surprise that the company is especially good at, for example, deep-sea oil exploration, production in polar regions, or transportation of liquefied natural gas (LNG) from remote areas. That, too, works in a self-reinforcing way: because Shell can create economies of scale in these kinds of projects, it can learn more quickly and extend its advantage over its competitors. "For example, you have a discussion about the question: if this specific technology is used in Syria, why can't we use it in other countries in the Middle East?" says Shell chief technology officer Gerald Schotman. "That's when economies of scale come into play. To me, scale does not only mean how big a project is, it's also about transferring knowledge, insights and opportunities from one part of the company to another. It's about integrating technology to use it to the fullest; and bringing it together in one organization makes a big difference, I think, in creating competitive advantage".[6]

---

[6]  J. Parshall (2011). 'Shell: Leadership Built on Innovation and Technology'. *Journal of Petroleum Technology*, January.

Shell promotes this spreading of knowledge and technology in various ways. The expats, for example, have traditionally been an important means of spreading know-how, because they work in ever-changing configurations in different locations. In the field of knowledge management, too, Shell is pushing the boundaries of the possible in order to maximize its use within the organization. As far back as the early 1980s, for example, Shell was already recording at 15-minute intervals for every well being drilled in the world, what tool configurations were being used, under what conditions and at what rate of progress. This created a wealth of information on which every employee involved in drilling could draw.

However, an important difference with smaller and more focused organizations is that it is easier for larger companies to lose sight of the core competency that first made them iconic. Short-term perspectives can gain the upper hand, especially when investors put the pressure on the management. We saw the consequences of this at Toyota, Steinway and Shell. Pride is a human failing, and when times are good, it is easy to think that anything is possible. It is the responsibility of senior leaders to keep this in check and to steer clear of markets where the company does not possess the unique competencies it needs to beat the competition. In other words, aspiration and competency must carry the same common thread and be relevant to the market. Someone who saw that better than anyone is A.G. Lafley, former CEO of Proctor & Gamble (P&G), the iconic marketeer that distributes global brands such as Pampers, Pringles, Gillette and Always:

> "A telling example for me personally is the case of Tide. In 1983, I had been with the company for six years, and was given the Tide brand to manage, the company's largest US brand and second largest worldwide. At the time, the market share was 21%, and we had discussions up to the chairman of the company about what the right laundry strategy should be. The pressure from above was to diversify into totally new brands and categories. Probably once per decade P&G goes off into a foray of 'let's create totally new categories and brands from scratch.' Then we return to find growth closer to the core. But, for a while, we milked Tide to pay for these forays into new areas, all of which, of course, failed.
>
> I was a voice crying in the wilderness: just give me one dollar for every ten I spent elsewhere, and I will find growth out of Tide. And we did. Between 1983 and 1993, we had grown Tide from a 21% share to a 30%

share and expanded the market. I believe the responsibility of a leading brand is to care for the market and to make sure it does not commoditize. Today the Tide share is 38% in the US and 47% in Canada. A target of 50% is not unreasonable. The basic product has led to a continuous stream of new adjacent opportunities ranging from Liquid Tide to Tide with Bleach to product upgrades with enzymatic stain removers. Sixty years of Tide and sixty years of upgrades and expansions from the core."[7]

Companies with iconic aspirations must therefore remain focused on what exactly it is that makes them good – their iconic competency or competencies - and achieve growth in those areas where they can use that competency to make a unique difference. The next company we shall look at, Danaher, does not seem at first sight to have learned this lesson: they make all sorts of things, from sockets to microscopes. But there is a system to it, a competency that is iconic in its industry.

# Danaher: Perfecting Newly Acquired Companies

Danaher is one of the best-performing conglomerates of recent decades.[8] This company takes over other companies that have underperforming manufacturing operations, and improves their performance using its Danaher Business System (DBS), which was inspired by the Toyota Production System. The sectors that Danaher operates in are carefully chosen growth markets, with a clear potential for DBS improvements and with opportunities for Danaher to become the market leader. Danaher is currently active in more than 80 sectors including dentists' apparatus, machines for analysing water, and professional tools. In investor and consulting circles, Danaher has an iconic status due to its ability to radically improve the performance of newly-acquired companies in a short time and create an enormous amount of value in the process, and yet the company is unknown to the general public. This is largely a conscious choice: Danaher prefers to fly below the radar and simply do what it is good at: buying up manufacturers,

---

[7] C. Zook (2004). *Beyond the Core*. Boston: Harvard Business School Press.

[8] Zook & Allen (2012).

merging them and improving their performance. The company and its executives are generally media shy. Founders and board members Steven and Mitchell Rales have not spoken to the media for 25 years.[9]

The Rales brothers started their company in the early 1980s as a vehicle for leveraged buy-outs (LBOs): they gained control of companies using largely loaned money. As it turned out, many of these LBOs went bust in the 1980s and 1990s, burdened by too much debt. However, Danaher soon went off in a different direction and devoted much more time and energy than did LBO companies to making operational improvements to the companies in its portfolio, and to paying off their debts. Around 1988, the Rales brothers noticed that one of their subsidiaries, Jacobs Vehicle Systems, was achieving rapidly improving results with *kaizen*, a set of techniques inspired by Toyota for achieving continuous improvement. They decided to apply these techniques to all their subsidiaries, and so the Danaher Business System (DBS) was born. With that, Danaher became one of the first American companies to become *lean*, and since then this philosophy has become deeply anchored in the company's DNA. "There are a lot of companies where if you win ten-nine, nobody wants to talk about the nine points the competitor scored. We'll celebrate the win, but we'll talk about 'How did we give up nine runs? Why didn't we score twelve?'"[10]

Four Ps stand at the core of DBS: *people, plan, process* and *performance.* These four are rigorously applied to every new and existing subsidiary in order to continuously improve the manufacturing process.[11] DBS can be regarded as a prefabricated circle of competence that is routinely implemented in newly-acquired companies,

In terms of *people*, for example, Danaher maintains a strict human-resource policy to retain and develop the best. Before a new company is taken over, an evaluation is made of the quality of the incumbent management by means of discussions with the board members. In the first weeks and months after the takeover, each individual's performance and desire to

---

[9]  B. Hindo (2007). 'A Dynamo Called Danaher'. *BusinessWeek*, 19 February.

[10]  Hindo (2007).

[11]  B. Anand, D.J. Collis & S. Hood (2008). *Danaher Corporation.* Harvard Business School case study.

improve are again closely examined, and those who are not expected to make a good fit with Danaher and DBS are asked to leave. The company replaces them as quickly as possible with new talent, for example with managers from other Danaher subsidiaries who have proven their ability to succeed and are very familiar with DBS.

In the *planning* phase the management of the newly-acquired company get together with the Danaher board to make a strategic plan to maximize the potential of the company. In fact, the newly-acquired company is provided with a new absolute aspiration through which iconic results are guaranteed, because its starting point is no longer the result of previous years but the potential that has yet to be achieved. "It is only after the deal is completed, and the bankers and lawyers are out of the room, that we can have an honest strategic conversation with management. At that point, we throw out the 180-page strategy manuals and create a plan for the new acquisition that is due within 100 days of purchase, and that is intended to produce a shared long-term vision. No sacred cows are left unchallenged, and our due-diligence findings are shared with the company."

The third P, *process*, is about how DBS is introduced to new managers. This is how the newly-acquired company is formed into a top team that is able to produce iconic results. The new managers are put through a week-long training session followed by a *kaizen* session of another week in one of the factories to dicuss in very concrete terms how DBS can improve the running of the company – often, pre-specified goals are set, such as *halving* the necessary space. These sessions are facilitated by managers who already have experience with DBS improvements, and Danaher's CEO always personally attends for a whole day to give training. Furthermore, up to a dozen operational managers are often sent on a tour of Danaher factories worldwide to be completely immersed in how DBS works in practice. The most important goal is that they become part of the *kaizen* DNA and that striving for continuous improvement becomes second nature.

Finally, *performance* is sustained with the help of the Policy Deployment, a means to translate a very limited number of strategic priorities into concrete actions, and over time to measure whether the goals are being achieved. This is how continuous feedback, which is so important for the circle of competence, is given in line with the newly-defined absolute aspiration. The starting point is always formed by the most important goals for strategic breakthroughs for the coming three to five years. These goals can include anything from finance (such as profit margin) to competitive position (market share) to quality (customer satisfaction) and to human resources (percentage of senior management vacancies filled internally). For each subsidiary, the two, three or four most important goals are determined separately, depending on the specific strategic situation of the subsidiary in question. These long-term goals are then translated into annual targets for the coming year and specific actions. For each action, it is agreed who will be responsible and how their progress will be measured as the year passes. The Policy Deployment programmes are made first for each subsidiary as a whole, after which the necessary goals and actions are further specified in comparable documents for each department and factory. In this way, strategic goals are translated into extremely concrete actions for every manager, and with pre-determined methods for measuring their progress.

Like the RCO, Danaher has the equivalent of a conductor in a complementary leadership role. This is because there is one group of people who are responsible for the implementation of the four Ps, the Danaher Business System Office (DBSO). This is a group of about 50 people who make sure that DBS is implemented in newly-acquired companies and continues to work effectively in the existing subsidiaries. In many companies, coordinating functions such as this are regarded with suspicion. Not at Danaher: working in the DBSO is considered a highly prestigious role, as it allows those that do it to develop an extensive knowledge of the company as well as a large network, and is often a springboard to securing a top position within Danaher. The DBSO also provides documentation and training in the more than 50 tools that currently make up DBS, and which are used to achieve the goals of the Policy Deployment programmes. Just like a conductor, the DBSO fills a complementary leadership role in helping to get the best out of the company.

Thanks to DBS, Danaher has grown in the last 30 years – under only three CEOs – into a company of more than 50,000 people and with over $20 billion in turnover. Danaher often achieves an improvement of 5% to 10% in the profit margin of companies it takes over. The return on equity that this growth and improvement in profit margin have achieved is phenomenal: an average of 20% to 25% per year over the past few decades.[12]

# Systems for Managing Competency

Like Shell, Danaher has one clear core competency – acquiring and operationally improving manufacturers. This competency is managed by a carefully selected team of a few hundred managers who continue to develop themselves. The four Ps form Danaher's version of the circle of competence. The parts have slightly different names and are structured slightly differently, but all the elements of the circle are visible: from rigorous selection (firing of managers who do not fit) to continuous talent management (DBS training) and from continuous feedback (KPIs[13] with regular follow-up) to absolute aspiration (goals for strategic breakthroughs in Policy Deployment).

The Danaher example also shows that companies often need to provide their own continuous feedback, as they don't have reviewers reporting on whether or not iconic performance has been achieved. This feedback is provided by a management system set up to manage the competency well. A system such as this is a valuable addition to the annual budget cycle that is leading in many companies. In their renowned *Harvard Business Review* article *Who Needs Budgets?*, Hope and Fraser draw on a 1998 study that reveals companies spend an average of more than 25,000 man-days on the budgeting process for every billion dollars of revenue. This means that companies spend an enormous amount of time on a process that is primarily focused on short-term results, instead of long-term competencies. In this respect, Danaher's Policy Deployment (PD) offers an excellent alternative for (or an addition to) the budgeting process. It is a simple system that gives managers the means to make a huge company manageable, while it obliges them also to manage for the long term. Former CEO H. Lawrence Culp Jr. describes the system like this:

> "'Policy Deployments' don't only involve the more senior managers; they are also translated into what they mean for the rest of the organization. If, for example, a part of a company has as its goal to double research productivity, then a PD goal could be set up to improve the research processes. Next, that goal could set in motion a series of other goals for the different constituent parts of the research department.

---

[12]  Zook & Allen (2012).

[13]  Key performance indicators.

We keep track of the PD goals on a single sheet of paper. Progress towards the goals is colour-coded: red is *off-track*, green is *on-track*, yellow is a question mark. Of course, red lights always get the most attention, but we don't always start with them – sometimes we start by talking about the green lights, to be sure they really are green. For the red lights we look at what the underlying causes of the problems are, and we have five 'why' questions that help us understand what needs to change and suggest concrete actions. The number of red lights for a part of a company is in itself not important, but it's not acceptable for lights to stay red for too long.

PD discussions are really not the same as 'management by numbers', as some people think. It's an iterative process where we start with the figures, then talk through the process, and then go back to the figures. Good performance is not just about having your figures in order – the most important thing is understanding how those figures were achieved. We're probably just as focused on numbers as any other company, but we combine that focus with a Toyota-like desire to continually improve the way we run the company. In the end, the most important thing about the PD process is getting techniques and processes working to put the figures right. Red lights can be a good thing, because they help to develop processes for the long term. Alternatively, we would also be very worried if all the lights were on green, because that would mean there was no more room for improvement."[14]

The power of PD is that it combines 'hard' figures with 'soft' discussion, and furthermore obliges managers to prioritize between the short and the long term – as opposed to the budget process, which all too often favours short-term optimisation at the cost of the long term. PD also obliges managers to be very clear and selective in setting priorities for the coming years; only initiatives that could produce breakthrough results are included as PD goals. Finally, PD ensures that strategic plans can indeed be implemented, because every initiative comes with concrete actions attached, with people assigned responsibility for achieving them and with benchmarks agreed against which progress can be measured.

Shell, too, has an extensive system for effectively managing the long-term view. Given the core competency of Shell engineers – carrying out the most challenging oil and gas projects in the world – it's not surprising that the company has set up effective systems to continue to develop its people. "In fact, for decades, Shell has had a sophisticated system for nurturing our core technical, commercial and functional skills," says Hugh Mitchell, Shell's chief human resources and corporate officer. "One priority is to retain close oversight of employees with the most sought-after skills. This allows us to manage all aspects of their career journeys, from graduate recruitment to pay and performance management. In particular, we need to ensure that our technically skilled employees are globally mobile. So we are preserving a strong pool of expatriate employees, amid fierce cost pressures across the industry. This allows us to continue training our engineers on foreign assignments, while maintaining a strong global stock of skills."[15] The expats play another important role. The size of this group and their relatively great mobility make them highly effective in carrying out the Shell way of working worldwide, and that specific knowledge can easily spread through the organization.

One of the systems that has been further developed in recent years is Current Estimated Potential (CEP). Every two years, CEP is used to make an estimate of employees' leadership potential based on three criteria: capabilities, results and relations. "Each part of the company has done the exercise to different timetables and somewhat different standards of execution," says Mike Conway, vice president of resourcing and development. "So 2008 is the first year that we will really have a single, consistent group-wide execution of a CEP exercise."[16]

In addition to CEP, the company also has other standardized systems to maintain a good overview of its talent. "We have a very clear line of sight from the top to the bottom of the organization," says Mitchell. "All 3,500 colleagues in HR report to the HR function, and not to the part of the company to which they are attached. And all important staffing decisions are made by a team of ten senior managers."

---

[14] Anand et al. (2008).

[15] H. Mitchell (2011). 'Linking talent strategies with business goals'. *Economist Talent Management Summit,* speech on 9 June 2011, http://www.shell.com/global/aboutshell/media/speeches-and-webcasts/2011/mitchell-london-09062011.html, retrieved on March 1 2013.

[16] M. Butteriss (2008). *Coaching Corporate MVPs: Challenging and Developing High-Potential Employees.* Mississauga, Ontario: John Wiley & Sons Canada.

# Disruptive Changes

In Chapter Four we discussed the need that organizations have not only to continually develop themselves, but also to adapt themselves to change where necessary (see the section on 'Tradition vs. Innovation'). In this respect, companies often find themselves in a different situation to sports teams, orchestras and restaurants. There are sectors of industry where change is so disruptive that few companies survive it, however iconic these companies were. Clayton Christensen of the Harvard Business School wrote his classic book *The Innovator's Dilemma* about this phenomenon.[17] He claims that most successful companies find few problems fitting technological *improvements* into their products and services, even if they happen very quickly. However, what is really disruptive is when change causes performance to *deteriorate*, at least at first. One of his examples is the transition from mainframe and mini-computers to home computers and personal computers (PCs). PCs of course were much less capable than their bigger brothers, and in the early days (the 1970s) could do so little that there was only a small market of hobby users available to them. For this reason, the computer giants of the time – IBM, Digital Equipment Corporation (DEC), Hewlett Packard (HP), Wang and many others – did not recognize the PC as a threat for the customer segment they served: large, rich companies who needed far more computing power than the PC could offer. However, the computing power offered by PCs grew much more quickly than the demand for computing power of large companies, and in the course of the 1980s the inevitable moment came when companies could get along just fine with the much cheaper and easier to use PCs. However, by that time it was too late for most computer manufacturers, because they were too far behind in PC technology. HP and IBM are two of the few that ultimately survived.

The dilemma that Christensen refers to in the title of his book is that effective managing during times of continuous technological improvement does not work when it comes to the *disruptive change* brought by new technologies which, at first, perform worse. Managers of large, successful companies often listen carefully to their customers' desire for technologies that improve their products, increase their margins and increase the size of their

---

[17] C.M. Christensen (1997). *The Innovator's Dilemma: When New Technologies Cause Great Firms to Fail.* Boston: Harvard Business School Press.

potential market. The problem with (once) disruptive technologies such as the PC, the transistor and the digital camera, however, is that these technologies in the early days are completely unknown to customers, are still very costly and often serve small niche markets because their performance leaves a lot to be desired – precisely the attributes that make disruptive technologies unattractive to managers of large companies. To put it boldy: should you listen to what your customer wants, or instead try your luck with new and possibly promising technologies? This is the dilemma.

The answer that Christensen gives is that companies and industries that may have to deal with disruptive technologies should at least be open to change, even if it might turn their business world upside down. Next, they must set up small, separate subsidiaries to develop these technologies. This also ensures that the competency that makes the company iconic can continue to operate normally and be improved upon, until the day may come when the subsidiary with the disruptive technology can take over the helm. This is roughly how things went at IBM, twice even. First, the PC department left the mainframe business far behind. More recently, the service organization (originally part of the sales department) has become IBM's core activity, while IBM has sold its PC division to the Chinese company Lenovo.

Having said that, dealing with disruptive technology still remains one of the most difficult strategic problems. It requires successful companies – at the right moment – to let go of an iconic competency, and to use it to develop a new one. IBM at least shows that this is possible – but there are not so many examples of other companies that have managed to do the same. A comforting thought is perhaps that, in most cases, the demise of iconic companies has not been due to disruptive technological changes but rather to unbridled growth, losing sight of what they are good at, or ceasing to innovate, or a combination of all three. Jim Collins, for example, finds in his research that "organizational decline is largely self-inflicted, and recovery largely within our own control".[18] This was certainly true of the most important examples of failure (temporary or otherwise) in this book: think of Steinway, Toyota, the Globetrotters, and Shell. They were successful as long as they used the nine elements of the circle of competence to focus on remaining iconic in their competency and, when a temporary crisis did strike, they were able to pick up the same circle again remarkably quickly.

# CHAPTER 8

# ICONIC COMPETENCE IN THE AGE OF INFORMATION

Institute for Advanced
Study, Princeton

This chapter discusses
the role of iconic
organizations in the
information age and
their relationship to
open collaborative
networks such as
Wikipedia. We
demonstrate how these
two organizational
forms are both
important in their own
way, and how open
collaborative networks
can even reinforce
iconic competence.

In this chapter, we deal with the role of icons in the age of information. Are the strict selection procedures of iconic organizations still relevant at a time of far-reaching democratization of knowledge and ways of working together? Can informal social networks, supported by technology, solve business problems just like real consultants? Will Shell soon be competing with oil rigs set up with the help of knowledge gathered by a collaborative network?

We will be asking ourselves what can differentiate iconic organizations from open, social collaborative networks, which use information technology to exploit "The Wisdom of Crowds"[1]. We will discuss the role of both – selection of individuals versus selection of ideas – and how they can reinforce one another.

Wikipedia shows how powerful open collaborative networks can be. This encyclopaedia, started in 2001, is much more extensive and much cheaper than the iconic *Encyclopaedia Britannica*. Wikipedia is so successful that in 2012, the last printed edition of the *Encyclopaedia Britannica* appeared after a history of 244 years.[2] Although the quality of Wikipedia is less consistent than that of the *Encyclopaedia Britannica*, it is more than 50 times bigger and includes many clickable references through which more information and pointers about a subject can be found. A not uncontroversial comparison by *Nature* magazine in 2005 revealed that for the natural science subjects, which were written largely by amateurs, Wikipedia contained four mistakes per article versus three mistakes per article in the *Encyclopaedia Britannica*, which was produced by several Nobel Prize winners and a team of 4,000 experts.[3]

Wikipedia is a clear example of just how much modern-day information technology has expanded and optimized the capacity that is available to us for achieving a particular result. So much so, in fact, that a very varied group of A, B and C players can achieve a result which, in parts, can compete with what the most iconic organizations can produce. But the question is whether open collaborative networks can generate the same capacity to redefine the possible and innovate as leading and iconic organizations.

In order to understand what role iconic competencies can continue to play in the future alongside these collaborative networks, let us take a look at the example of the Institute for Advanced Study at Princeton. This institute has been home to many legendary scientists, including John von Neumann (one of the founders of the modern computer), Kurt Gödel (who shook the foundations of mathematics), J. Robert Oppenheimer (the 'father of the atom bomb'), and, of course, Albert Einstein. The following is taken from a conversation with Robbert Dijkgraaf, the Dutch mathematical physicist and director of the institute, who speaks about the magic of Princeton and its role in the future.

# Princeton: 'Heaven on Earth for Scientists'[4]

Abraham Flexner set up the Institute for Advanced Study in 1930 (this was the same Flexner we encountered in Chapter Six when discussing Johns Hopkins because, after extensive study, he praised that institute as a role model for medical science). "The institute should be small and flexible." Flexner said. "It should be a haven where scholars and scientists could regard the world and its phenomena as their laboratory without being carried off in the maelstrom of the immediate. It must be simple, comfortable and quiet without becoming a remote monastery; it must not shy away from any problem. It must not come under pressure from any side whatsoever which may be prejudiced for or against a particular solution for a problem that is being studied; it must offer the facilities that are needed to do fundamental research into the unknown. The faculty must be given complete intellectual freedom and be entirely free from any responsibility or cares."

The institute stills lives up to this vision today. With 50 permanent professors (including emeriti) and around 200 visiting scholars each year, the institute is still "small and flexible" – those present always take lunch

---

[1]   *The Wisdom of Crowds: Why the Many Are Smarter Than the Few and How Collective Wisdom Shapes Business, Economies, Societies and Nations*, James Surowiecki, 2004

[2]   Various. *Encyclopædia Britannica*. Wikipedia English-language edition, http://en.wikipedia.org/wiki/Encyclop%C3%A6dia_Britannica.

[3]   Jim Giles (2005). *Nature*, vol. 438, December.

[4]   Quoted from a member of Princeton IAS, see Institute for Advanced Study (2009). *Report of the Decadal Review Committee of the Board of Trustees*, internal publication. Princeton, NJ: Institute for Advanced Study.

together. It also remains completely independent. Uniquely among scientific institutions of its size, Princeton does not accept any donations that come with conditions attached – including therefore government subsidies for specific research.

The interview with Dijkgraaf turns almost automatically to the institute's circle of competence. "With only 50 professors, every appointment counts," he says about finding the right people. "We want to retain the best scientists. But we don't want a 'trophy cabinet' of top academics at the end of their career, but rather researchers who show the greatest promise for the future. We go for the best results, and that means that we also have to dare to take big risks. Using all the information we can get from our network of scientists, we try to optimize the relationship between risk and reward – a bit like when you invest in shares. But the fact that we go for best results means that we sometimes have to take it on the nose if an appointment doesn't work out. However, that said, by far the majority of the scientists at the institute are successful and undertake extremely innovative research."

What also typifies the institute is the way it 'seduces' the best people into wanting to stay. That is actually what happened to Dijkgraaf himself. He never thought he would want to become the director of the Institute for Advanced Studies, until one day, while on vacation in New York, he accepted an invitation to dine with a number of trustees, the people who provide funding for the institute.[5] After the dinner, one of the trustees offered to take Dijkgraaf on his private jet for a look around Princeton, "and we didn't want to miss a flight like that". The conversation with the trustees set Dijkgraaf's mind working, and we all know the result.

Those who make it through the institute's rigorous selection are given completely free rein to undertake innovative research, without any form of limitation. Nobody has any teaching obligations, citation scores are not catalogued, and everyone earns the same salary. And yet everyone feels an enormous sense of responsibility towards themselves, their colleagues, and science in general to come up with innovative ideas. "This culture is reproduced not only by the academic staff, but also by the trustees and the support staff," says Dijkgraaf. "The trustees are often attached to the institute for a lifetime. Of course they help by providing financial support, but also by strengthening a sense of continuity and focus. Even the support staff feel extremely committed to the institute. Some families have been working with us here for generations, and are friends with each other. And not so long ago there was a snowstorm – and the caretakers were up at three o'clock in the morning, removing fallen trees and clearing snow for 24 hours non-stop, just so that they could minimize the inconvenience to scientists at the institute."

Apart from the freedom from cares that the institute offers, the chance meetings with the greatest minds in different disciplines and generations of scientist have been crucial to the value of the institute. In 1972, for instance, the mathematician Hugh Montgomery happened to be having tea in the Fuld Hall at Princeton with the physicist Freeman Dyson (a living legend who is still regularly to be found there). Montgomery told Dyson that he was working on the Riemann hypothesis, one of the greatest – as yet unsolved – problems of science. He had had an important insight into the distribution of zero points of the Riemann function, and wrote it up on the blackboard. As he was writing, Dyson's eyes widened in amazement: this was precisely the formula that he had discovered for the distribution of energy levels of heavy nuclei! In this way, one of the greatest connections was made between mathematics and physics in the twentieth century.

The peace, the freedom, the number of great scholars all in one place – all this creates a "magical atmosphere", in the words of Dijkgraaf. "But the fact that Oppenheimer's secretary still works at the institute, for example, also adds to the magic. Or the buildings: every scientist who has lived in the house of Albert Einstein has gone on to win a Nobel Prize. Or the tradition of three different cookies with every cup of tea. And in a certain way you do feel the personalities of greats such as Gödel and Oppenheimer still resonating through." Here, too, we recognize the ship of Theseus.[6]

---

[5]  M. van der Heijden (2011). 'Making my world smaller again'. *NRC Handelsblad*, 24 December.

[6]  See Chapter Four, section on 'Innovation rooted in tradition'.

Einstein and colleagues Yukawa, Wheeler and Bhabha stroll in the park of Princeton

But Princeton again has that paradoxical combination of tradition and innovation that characterizes icons. "The institute has never been afraid of taking risks and doing things in radically different ways," says Dijkgraaf. "In the 1940s, for example, the institute made an enormous investment in building the world's first programmable computer. And Oppenheimer appointed George Kennan as professor, even though he wasn't even a scientist – but he grew into an icon. With this history, and unfettered by bureaucracy, we therefore have no choice but to become the most progressive institute in the scientific world and to embrace the latest information technology. It is an important subject for us, a process that – just like every other important decision made at Princeton – runs bottom-up. For example, we are looking at how we can keep the 6,000 scientists who come here as guests more closely involved, thanks to the latest technology.

But even in a changing world, we will continue to live by our core values of complete academic freedom and a liberating sense of peace and quiet in a world where everything is supposed to move ever faster. Our goal is ultimately to take the first steps in very broad scientific terrain – this is what we have always done, and this is what we always want to continue to do."

How is the institute doing today? "One of my most important measures for our iconicity is the percentage of people who say 'yes' out of the very small number of post-doctoral researchers that we make an offer to," says Dijkgraaf. "Last year over 95% accepted our offer. This year it was 100%."

## The Eternal Value of Icons

The protection that Princeton offers from pressure and daily cares, combined with the highest concentration of top scientists in the world (which facilitates unplanned meetings that lead to discoveries of global importance) are characteristics that make the institute unique, especially in our day and age. It is this kind of characteristic that makes it impossible to replace teams of top specialists in a certain field with any technology whatsoever, and which will continue to give them their right to exist.

The "curse of knowledge" is perhaps one of the most important reasons why iconic teams have a right to exist. Brothers Chip and Dan Heath explain this curse in their book *Made to Stick* by means of an experiment with drummers and listeners, carried out by Elizabeth Newton at Stanford University in 1990.[7] In this experiment, a drummer is asked to beat out the tune of a well-known song, such as 'Happy Birthday' – without further sound. This turned out to be surprisingly difficult: only 3 of the 120 listeners guessed the right tune. The drummers, on the other hand, estimated the chance that they had successfully transmitted the tune at at least 50%. The reason was that while they were drumming, they sang the song in their heads. They could no longer 'undo' this knowledge, and they could therefore no longer imagine how difficult it would be for others to guess the song if all they could hear was the rhythm and not the melody. When we know what we mean, it is only with great difficulty that we

---

[7]  C. Heath & D. Heath (2007). *Made to Stick*. London: Random House.

can imagine that others possibly do not understand it. That is the curse of knowledge.

The curse of knowledge can give iconic organizations, consisting as they do of A players, an advantage over more open collaborative networks, which consist of a large group of people that, by definition, also contains B and C players. In open collaborative networks, the B and C players in particular will understand each other only partially, due to the curse of knowledge in combination with the relatively short time that they have been interacting together. There is simply no room for the long learning curve that a truly iconic organization experiences on its climb to unparalleled results and iconicity. Members of an iconic team know each other through and through and only need a nod and a wink because they have spent so much time together. In the Concertgebouw Orchestra, each member is constantly adjusting to the others in order to form a single entity, mostly without a single word being said. Likewise, the best Michelin-starred kitchens can be recognized by the fact that chefs hardly speak to each other while they are cooking. Because people in iconic teams support each other for years on end, they are able to benefit from enormously efficient communication, which cannot be achieved without such a strong team. This efficient communication serves as a remedy against the curse of knowledge, and it is therefore an important part of the learning curve that is needed to become iconic.

Moreover, the chance of fruitful meetings between A-players is much greater at, say, Princeton or the Pixar campus than on an internet forum. "Predictability is the worst thing that can happen to you as a scientist," says Dijkgraaf. "If you want to arrive at truly innovative insights, you have to take a sideways step every now and again – but that is very hard. Because of the high degree of interaction at the institute, our visiting scholars regularly end up doing something different to what they originally expected. That often leads to truly innovative, unexpected insights."

In addition to these *differences* there is another important characteristic that iconic organizations *share* with the best open collaborative networks: bringing people together who all strive to achieve a truly shared goal. In iconic organizations, absolute aspiration to achieve a shared goal is an important part of the circle of competence, and it forms a basic ingredient for the common thread that runs through the circle. In a thesis written for the INSEAD business school, Mik van den Noort, a leadership coach who has worked a great deal with the Concertgebouw Orchestra, concludes that the success of an orchestra is largely down to the collective longing within the orchestra to make beautiful music and create the conditions which make this possible.[8]

That is an important difference with many non-iconic organizations. Nowadays, any self-respecting company has a mission statement with which it hopes to motivate its employees towards a common goal, but this is often no more than a regularly modified sloganesque kind of text, which management formulated to summarize their strategy, usually in words that the employees cannot do anything with (the curse of knowledge). It is therefore hardly surprising that these kinds of text are viewed tongue in cheek, that they change little in behaviour on the shop floor, and that people wait patiently until the next new corporate slogan comes along.

Iconic organizations, on the other hand, do not showcase their mission, but have internalized it as a truly shared goal. During our tour of the Steinway piano factory in Hamburg, we see an employee polishing a piano leg. He pauses for a moment, and explains to us how important it is that he always holds the surface flat against the polishing wheel, and that the process of lacquering and polishing is repeated seven times. "That's why Steinway black is much deeper than that of other piano makers." Everyone at Steinway feels personally responsible for realizing their absolute aspiration: to make the best concert grand pianos in the world. At Princeton, everyone is intrinsically motivated to come up with groundbreaking ideas. At McKinsey, every consultant hopes to find the breakthrough insights for their client. At elBulli, the chefs wanted to surprise the guests with the most delightful and unusual dishes. These are not missions that are imposed from above, but which are lived up to within the organization.

An open source collaboration project such as Wikipedia is quite closely comparable to iconic organizations in that both have a truly shared goal. Wikipedia now brings together more than 77,000 people each month,

[8]   M. van den Noort (2011). *A study of leadership in the Royal Concertgebouw Orchestra.* INSEAD CCC Masters Thesis:

[9]   Wikipedia, http://en.wikipedia.org/wiki/Wikipedia:About, accessed on 18 March 2013.

all actively helping to make the knowledge available in the world quickly accessible.[9] The writers of the articles do not receive any form of financial reward; they are driven purely by their intrinsic motivation. Another example is the Linux operating system, developed by programmers across the entire world. Thanks to its flexibility and stability, this system is often used in professional servers – the majority of the 500 most powerful supercomputers run on Linux.[10]

The goals of Linux or of Wikipedia are ideal for open collaboration, because they require input from a large number of people who can all work separately, and because no truly innovative insights need to be developed. But for true innovation in a specific area of study, an iconic competence such as that found at Princeton is much more suitable. Iconic organizations and open collaboration therefore fulfill complementary roles.

Some organizations even use the best of both worlds: there are icons that strengthen their competence through open collaboration. Proctor & Gamble is a good example. This company has always been iconic in the field of product development, but about ten years ago it realized that there was probably more relevant product innovation capacity and knowledge outside P&G than inside.[11] It was also clear that developers need a certain length of time to develop specific skills. The company realized that in a rapidly changing environment with a variable need for development skills, development capacity had to be found outside P&G in order to bring an optimized stream of new and innovative products to market. The company did this with its Connect + Develop programme. This initiative brings a variety of parties together with innovations, development competencies, marketing, access to distribution and means of production in order to create more value for consumers more quickly. The similarity between Wikipedia and P&G's Connect + Develop programme is that both achieve a significant optimization of the deployed capacity, thanks to the open nature of the initiative. Where P&G goes even further than Wikipedia is that Connect + Develop also provides a way to make money for all parties involved.

The collaboration methods made possible by information technology therefore offer fantastic opportunities for iconic organizations to interact much more closely with knowledge, skills and the public in a broad sense. We have already seen, for example, how Princeton tries to use technology to involve its 6,000 alumni much more closely in the institute's knowledge development. The Concertgebouw Orchestra, too, is experimenting with new technologies, such as the RCO Universe, as a way of attracting more people to classical music. An example is a pilot with an app based around the Koningsnacht concert featuring the British artist Fink, which uses 360-degree filming techniques to enable users to sit 'virtually' between the musicians.

Mariss Jansons puts it as follows: "We live together for music."[12] This feeling describes the essence of an iconic organization. New technologies make it possible to share this striving for beauty with an even greater number of people.

---

[10]  TOP500, http://www.top500.org/statistics/details/osfam/1, accessed on 4 April 2013.

[11]  L. Huston & N. Sakkab (2006). 'Connect and Develop: Inside Procter & Gamble's New Model for Innovation.' *Harvard Business Review*, March.

[12]  M. van den Noort (2011).

# FINAL WORD

We have written this book first and foremost as a source of inspiration. However, books are quickly forgotten and inspiration soon ebbs away, particularly if we start Monday morning with a full inbox, a long to-do list, endless meetings and perhaps frustrations about bureaucracy and inertia.

For this reason, we have written this final word in the form of a summary of the most important concepts, listed by chapter. Finally, we pose a number of questions for reflection.

# Chapter-by-chapter Summary

## 1. Magic on demand

- **Magic**: something that is very good, with a few extras (extraordinary); for example Mahler's Third Symphony at Carnegie Hall, blocks of curry with chicken sauce at elBulli, iPad.
- **Iconic**: generally recognized as leading by everyone in its field.
- **Iconic competence**: the ability to remain iconic for longer than deemed possible (e.g. a century).
- **Circle of Iconic Competence**: the sustained repetition of the circle: talent, team & time (and back to talent).

## 2. Talent

- **The right people**: top talent with the will and the skill to grow and fit in with the team.
- **Magnet for top talent**: a company that actively uses its iconic status to retain top talent; Steve Jobs: "A players want to work with A players and learn from them."
- **Rigorous selection**: selection of the right people through strict competence testing. Examples include the RCO auditions and the McKinsey case interviews.
- **Zero tolerance for non-performance**: letting go of people who structurally lower the performance level while remaining humane and offering help in case of temporary problems. Von Karajan:

"The back row of the second violins determines the quality of the orchestra."

- **Danger – lowering the standards**: lowering standards during times of talent shortage and reverting to recruiting B players to meet demand.

## 3. Team

- **Top team**: a team that adds to the qualities of each individual (1 + 1 = 3).
- **Continuous talent development**: development through intrinsic motivation (vs. external reward). Receiving confidence from the team to go for a perfect 10. Development by getting spare time to learn, teach, play in other team settings (e.g. chamber music).
- **Pure meritocracy**: a system in which the best performers are the most highly valued and rewarded; 'power through merit'. E.g. McKinsey: good ideas from junior consultants are taken into consideration.
- **Complementary leadership**: starting from the quality of the team and adding to it; Jansons: "A good orchestra doesn't need someone to keep time. It needs inspiration."
- **Danger – the curse of power**: Macbeth is a competent person in the wrong circumstances; don't create absolute power by concentrating it into a single pair of hands; go for distributed power instead (and design the governance accordingly).

## 4. Time

- **Unparalleled results over time**: unique level of achievement for longer than deemed possible, generally recognized by everyone in the field.
- **Continuous feedback**: giving and seeking feedback on an individual and team level; elBulli: continuing to taste; RCO: feedback through rehearsals, (guest) conductors; audience, reviewers. If opportunities for feedback are too limited, create ones. E.g. Steinway concert hall.
- **Innovation rooted in tradition**: striking the right balance between continuing to do what you are good at and going in search

of the new; for example, using computer technology at Steinway to improve on hundred-year-old designs.

- **Absolute aspiration**: an unceasing desire to improve on your last achievement; IKEA: *Most things remain to be done. A glorious future!*
- **Danger – when money takes centre stage**: example of Toyota, where the main priority to produce the best quality was replaced by an ambition to become the leader in the global market; returning to the quality DNA after problematic product recalls.

## 5. Organizing the Circle of Iconic Competence

- **Governance structure**: *Mitbestimmung* or co-determination with the aim of making the circle more robust: everyone feels responsible for the result and quality DNA is firmly anchored.
- **Social cohesion**: importance of informal interaction; RCO: 'solving petty irritations more easily while on tour; going for a beer afterwards'. Pixar: toilets only in central hall; Steinway Village.
- **Common thread**: between various organizations the parts of the circle of competence are the same, but the implementation is different; RCO: mutual trust, chameleon-like quality; Berlin Philharmonic: technical quality, faultless performance; Vienna Philharmonic: self-organization, *Wiener Schmelz*.

## 6. How the Virtuous Circle Begins

- **Phase One. Visionary leaders**: one or more determined leaders with a vision to produce iconic results. E.g. RCO; produces a huge leap in musical quality in Amsterdam, and is already recognized as iconic after only five years (*Handelsblad* newspaper article from 1893).
- **Phase Two. Implementing the circle of competence**: anchoring the absolute aspiration and reinforcing all elements of the circle; growing or breaking free of the visionary leaders and ensuring distributed leadership.
- **Phase Three. Iconic competence**: keeping the circle of iconic competence going; it often turns out to be resilient and robust, even after a temporary crisis (Harlem Globetrotters, Toyota, Steinway, Shell).

## 7. Icons of Industry

- **Iconic competence within a large company**: one or more main competencies on which the virtuous circle primarily operates; Shell: pushing the envelope in oil and gas exploration and production; Danaher: perfecting newly-acquired companies.
- **Systems for managing competency**: danger of the budgeting process – managing only for short-term profit; Danaher: Policy Deployment System makes long-term competency measurable – "the most important thing is understanding how the figures have been worked out".
- **Disruptive change**: IBM: servicing the sales organization is now the core activity; but organizational decline comes mostly from within, not as a result of external change.

## 8. Iconic Organizations in the Age of Information

- **Truly shared goal**: not about showcasing mission statements, but internalizing a shared purpose – applies both to iconic organizations and to successful open collaboration groups (such as Wikipedia); Jansons: "We live together for music."
- **Open collaboration groups**: contributions from many to a common goal, increasingly with the support of technology – Wikipedia, Linux, P&G Connect & Develop.
- **Iconic organization**: selected group of individuals who share an absolute aspiration to work together efficiently towards an innovative result – Princeton.

# Questions for reflection

- Do our customers and the general public see us as an iconic organization in our field?
- Do our people know what we want to become iconic in?
- Do we have the right people for our aspiration? Are some people holding us back? Can these people change, or do they need to leave?
- Does the team add to the individual qualities of the team members (1 + 1 = 3)?
- Does the team instill individuals with the confidence to go for a perfect ten?
- How pure is our meritocracy, do people up and down the hierarchy feel the same about this?
- Does everyone in the organization feel a sense of shared responsibility for the end product or service?
- Does our governance structure prevent too dominant leadership?
- How do we guarantee sufficient internal and external feedback?
- What is the relationship between financial and non-financial aspirations in our organizations?
- What makes people in our organization proud, and what stands in the way of this pride?
- Do our people remember those few remarkable successes, or do they never forget those very few failures?

# ACKNOWLEDGMENTS

We would like to thank the members of the Royal Concertgebouw Orchestra who shared their experience with such enthusiasm; in alphabetical order: Marc Daniël van Biemen, Christian van Eggelen, Louise Fresco, Conductor Emeritus Mariss Jansons, Jan Kouwenhoven, Jan Willem Loot, Johan van Maaren, Robert Reibestein, Herman Rieken, Jörgen van Rijen, Dominic Seldis, Jette Straub, Julia Tom, Maarten van Veen, Marja Verhoogt and Robert Waterman. Their passion has been contagious.

Further we thank all the others which we have interviewed and who gave us in-depth insights into iconic organisations, amongst others: Robbert Dijkgraaf of the Institute for Advanced Study in Princeton, Martin Grapengeter of Klinikum Bad Hersfeld, Hugo van Hulst who has worked for Cirque du Soleil, Dieter Flury of the Wiener Philharmoniker, Werner Husmann and Hartwig Kalb of Steinway, Bert Koopman of Het Financieele Dagblad, Chris Maene and Hans Vervenne of Piano's Maene, Fergus McWilliam and Pamela Rosenberg of the Berliner Philharmoniker, Jeroen van der Veer about his time with Shell, and Thiemo Wind of De Telegraaf.

We thank Anne Christin Erbe, Joel Fried, Martijn Voorvelt and the others of the Concertgebouw Orchestra that have read the manuscript and who tirelessly provided us with valuable annotations. Our gratitude equally goes to Mik van den Noort, independent leadership advisor, for her enthusiasm and valuable comments. Furthermore, many thanks to Marjolein Schulting who managed the agenda, booked rooms, printed chapters, forwarded data, and did much more to facilitate the authors.

As authors we thank the partners and colleagues of Benthurst & Co who believed in the book and helped in making it possible.

Xavier is grateful for the exchange of ideas he has with John Heller, Gert De Winter, Antonio Cano, Vincent Teekens and Charles Zijderveldt on building better and more authentic organizations. He furthermore thanks Dolf Balkema who taught him as an *industry hire* the consulting profession. And Nathalie, for her energy.

Gillis thanks all iconic and leading organisations, and all those who helped these in becoming what they are, for their inspiration and passion for pushing beyond the boundaries of the ordinary.

Jan thanks his wife Olga Beloborodova for the critical review of the manuscript.

Phebo thanks Chris Zook, partner with Bain & Company, as his mentor and teacher in conducting and writing strategy research. To conclude, he thanks his wife Truke Smoor for her support in swapping security for chasing dreams.

Our final word goes to Neal Woodcock who did an amazing job translating the book.

# LITERATURE LIST

Ariely, D., Gneezy, U., Loewenstein, G. & Mazar, N. (2005). *Large stakes and big mistakes.* Working paper series, Federal Reserve Bank of Boston, No. 05-11.

Chevalier, M. (1868) (red.). *Rapports du Jury International, Exposition Universelle de 1867 à Paris.* Tome deuxième, Groupe II, Classes 6 à 13. Parijs

Christensen, C.M. (1997). *The Innovator's Dilemma: When New Technologies Cause Great Firms to Fail.* Boston: Harvard Business School Press.

Collins, J. (2001). *Good to Great.* New York: HarperCollins.

Dolge, A. (1911). *Pianos and their Makers.* Covina, California: Covina Publishing Company.

Flothuis, M. & Giskes, J. (1989) (red.). *Waar bemoei je je mee: 75 jaar belangenstrijd van de Vereniging 'Het Concertgebouworkest'.* Zutphen: Walburg.

Gladwell, M. (2008). *Outliers: The Story of Success.* Londen: Penguin Books.

Gooley, D. (2004). *The Virtuoso Listz.* Cambridge: Cambridge University Press.

Gourville, J.T. & Lassiter III, J.B. (2000). *Steinway & Sons: Buying a Legend*. Boston, MA: Harvard Business School Publishing.

Grube, T. (2008). *Trip to Asia – Die Suche nach dem Einklang*. Boomtown Media International [dvd].

Hamel, G. & Breen, B. (2007). *The Future of Management*. Boston, MA: Harvard Business School Publishing.

Heath, C. & Heath, D. (2007). *Made to Stick*. Londen: Random House.

Hope, J. & Fraser, R. (2003). Who Needs Budgets?, *Harvard Business Review*, feb.

Isaacson, W. (2011). *Steve Jobs*. New York: Simon & Schuster.

Kamprad, I. (2007). *The Testament of a Furniture Dealer*. Delft: Inter IKEA Systems B.V.

Khalifa, M. (2012) (red.). *Bravo! 125 jaar Het Concertgebouw en Koninklijk Concertgebouworkest*. Amsterdam: Uitgeverij Balans.

Kotha, S. & Dunbar, R. (1997). *Steinway & Sons*. New York: Stern School of Business, NY University.

McGehee Harvey, A. & McKusick, V.A. (1989). *A Model of Its Kind: Volume 1 – A Centennial History of Medicine at Johns Hopkins.* Baltimore: Johns Hopkins University Press.

B. Niles (2007). *Note by Note. The making of Steinway L1037.* Real Fiction [dvd].

Parshall, J. (2011). Shell: Leadership Built on Innovation and Technology. *Journal of Petroleum Technology,* jan.

Peters, T. & Waterman, R.H. Jr. (1982). *In Search of Excellence: Lessons from America's Best-Run Companies.* New York: Harper & Row.

Pink, D.H. (2009). *Drive: The Surprising Truth About What Motivates Us.* New York: Riverhead Books.

Porter, M.E. (1996). What is Strategy?, *Harvard Business Review,* nov.-dec.

Van Royen, H.J. et al. (red.), *Historie en kroniek van het Concertgebouw en het Concertgebouworkest.* Zutphen: De Walburg Pers.

Singer, A. (1986). *Labor management relations at Steinway & Sons,* 1853–1896. New York: Garland.

Stadler, C. en Wältermann, P. (2012). *Die Jahrhundert-Champions.* Stuttgart: Schäffer-Poeschel Verlag.

Veysey, A. (1974). *Colin Meads All Black.* Auckland, Nieuw-Zeeland: William Collins.

Walker, A. (1983). *Franz Liszt: The Virtuoso Years, 1811-1847.* New York: Cornell University Press.

Wetzel, G. (2012). *El Bulli: Cooking in Progress.* Alive Mind [dvd].

Zook, C. (2004). *Beyond the Core.* Boston: Harvard Business School Press.

Zook, C. & Allen, J. (2012). *Repeatability: Build Enduring Businesses for a World of Constant Change.* Boston: Harvard Business Review Press.